STUDY GUIDE FOR
# INTRODUCTION TO BUSINESS

# STUDY GUIDE FOR
# INTRODUCTION TO BUSINESS
## A Contemporary View

FOURTH EDITION

**John A. Reinecke**
University of New Orleans

**William F. Schoell**
University of Southern Mississippi

**Alvin J. Williams**
University of Southern Mississippi

**Thomas S. O'Connor**
University of New Orleans

**Allyn and Bacon, Inc.**    Boston   London   Sydney   Toronto

The authors would like to acknowledge the
excellent editing and typing assistance of
Sarah Curry.

# CONTENTS

# TO THE STUDENT

WHAT YOU CAN GAIN FROM USE OF THE
*STUDY GUIDE*

Your first course in business lays the basic, essential foundation upon which you will build your understanding of the exciting world of business.  Putting forth your best effort to learn the material presented during this course will be beneficial both in your future business courses and in your career.  You will be better prepared for later courses and that alone will make them more interesting and relevant.  That, of course, is dependent on the fact that you will make the best possible use of your abilities.  Furthermore, a good understanding of this course will initiate thinking about where you may successfully fit into the business world.

This *Study Guide* will help you to make the best use of your valuable study time.  For best results you should use the *Study Guide* as a workbook to check your progress as you read the corresponding chapters in the text.  This will serve to indicate how well you understand the text material and also will point up areas that require additional review for you.

THE ORGANIZATION OF THE *STUDY GUIDE*

For each chapter in the text, there is a corresponding chapter in the *Study Guide*.  The format of each chapter is as follows:

1. Chapter Preview
2. Test Your Business Vocabulary
3. Programmed Review
4. Test Yourself (Multiple Choice)
5. Test Yourself (True-False)
6. Exercises

## Chapter Preview

These sections provide a preview of the corresponding chapter in the text. They give you some insight into the major topics that are discussed in the text chapter.

You may want to read these previews, along with the introductory comments in the text chapter, prior to reading the chapter. It is also a good idea to read the preview, along with the Summary and Look Ahead section at the end of the chapter in the text. Together they provide a useful approach to reviewing the content of each chapter.

## Test Your Business Vocabulary

Your job in these sections is to match key concepts from each chapter with phrases that describe or define each key concept. The correct answers to this self-test are given at the end of each chapter, along with page references to text discussion of the key concepts. For best results take this test after your first reading of the chapter. If you mismatch any pair, go back to the text and review.

You may attempt to read down the list of phrases and name or jot down the concept that fits each phrase before you look at the list of key concepts. Then follow the regular instructions for matching listed key concepts with the set of phrases.

## Programmed Review

In these sections you will find the objectives that are stated at the beginning of each chapter in the text. Following each of these learning objectives are one or more short exercises to help you test your mastery of the objectives. The pages in the text where the answers to these exercises appear are indicated at the end of each chapter.

These objectives tell you what you should be able to accomplish after reading each chapter in the text. Take the time to read these objectives before you read the text chapter. After you have read the chapter, complete the short exercises in the *Study Guide*. If you are unable to accomplish one or more of these exercises, review the relevant sections of the text chapter.

## Test Yourself (Multiple Choice)

In these sections you will attempt to select the best of several answers supplied to complete a statement or to answer a question. This self-test is similar to the type of exams your instructor may give. Correct answers are given at the end of each chapter, along with page references to relevant text discussion. Take this test after your first reading of the chapter. Go back and review the text, if you do not achieve a perfect score.

To test yourself in greater depth, try changing and rewording the questions or statements so that more than one of the choices becomes a correct response. Or you could reword and modify the choices so that all of them would fit the question or statement. This extra effort on your part should pay off in greater understanding and better grades on exams.


## Test Yourself (True-False)

These are statements that you will judge as being either <u>true</u> or <u>false</u>. If you believe one is false, determine why. The correct answers are given at the end of each chapter, along with page references to relevant text discussion. Take this exam after your first reading of the chapter. Go back and review the text, if you do not achieve a perfect score.

As an extra learning tool, you might also do the following: If you think that a given statement is false, try to rewrite it so that it would be true. Likewise, if you think that a given statement is true, try to rewrite it so that it would be false.


## Exercises

Each chapter in the *Study Guide* contains five exercises for you to complete. There are matching exercises, short answer essays, sentence completions, involvement exercises, crossword puzzles, word puzzles, and an incident with questions for you to answer. The answers and/or page references to relevant text discussion for two of these exercises are provided at the end of each chapter.

The answers to three of the exercises are not provided at the end of the chapter. Your instructor may ask you to complete and submit one or more of these three exercises for a grade. Even if you are not required to submit a particular exercise for a grade, it is a good idea to complete it in order to prepare yourself for exams.


## USING THE TEXTBOOK

To attain the maximum benefit from using the *Study Guide*, you should make the best use of your textbook. Here are a few suggestions.

1. When you begin each section, take time to read carefully the section introduction. It gives you an overall idea of what is discussed in that particular section. It also helps you to organize the material in preparation for study.
2. When you begin each chapter, read over the statements that tell you what you should be able to accomplish after studying each chapter. Do the same for the lists of key concepts. These study aids help you to know *in advance* what is most

important in the chapters.

3. Pay close attention to the words and sentences in boldface because they define the key concepts in each chapter. Notice that the key concepts are printed in the margin next to the definitions. All key concepts are also listed and defined in the glossary at the end of the text. If you have difficulty in understanding other business terms, check the glossary. Chances are that those terms are defined there.

4. Read and think about the material that is included in the boxes that appear throughout the text. Some of these boxes deal with real world business practices and some raise interesting, often controversial, topics for discussion. These boxes also demonstrate to you that business is not boring. It is lively and there is room for differences of opinion.

5. It is wise to begin considering the careers that are available in business. Each section discusses careers in business, both in terms of opportunities available and preparation for a career and in terms of a specific career profile of a person in the business world. This feature is designed to give you some idea of specific types of jobs and careers in business and to initiate thought concerning your own career.

6. The charts, graphs, and tables are important in summarizing and emphasizing material discussed in the chapters. Take the time to study them closely. See if you can "put into words" the meaning of the graphs.

7. Pay particular attention to the *Summary and Look Ahead* section for each chapter. It summarizes what the chapter is about and tells you what to expect in the next chapter.

8. The *For Review* questions near the end of each chapter are for review of the topics discussed in each particular chapter. The *For Discussion* questions focus on interesting issues that you can reflect upon and discuss. Try to develop thoughtful answers to each of these questions. Discuss them with your fellow students and others and be prepared to defend your answers.

9. The *Incidents* at the end of each chapter describe real business situations. Put yourself into the situation and answer the questions given. Discuss the incidents with your classmates.

10. There is a *Case Study* for each section of the text. These provide greater depth than the *Incidents*. The questions provided will stimulate you to think and make decisions that are very similar to the decisions managers face every day.


INTERPRETING GRAPHS AND OTHER CHARTS

Your *Introduction to Business* textbook presents a wide variety of illustrations that summarize facts and relationships important to business. Because some of these may be unfamiliar to you, we will present several examples here along with an explanation of their use.

Figure 1-1 deals with an important measure of the overall economy--Gross National Product (GNP). Instead of presenting actual numbers in table form, it presents numbers graphically. This means that a line is drawn to indicate the growth of that value over time (shown on the horizontal scale). The amounts for each year are read by comparing the heights of the line with the vertical scale at the left. This scale is measured in billions of dollars. Looking at the continuous line you can see that GNP was roughly $1,300 billion at the end of 1972 and about $3,000 billion near the end of 1981. This line simplifies the analysis of growth over time in order to compare relative size of GNP in different years. The dotted line shows the same scale, with a correction for inflation. This means that changes in GNP between 1973 and 1981 are corrected to adjust to changes in the value of the dollar. What remains is an indication of the change in real GNP during this time.

Figure 1-1.  Gross National Product of the United States

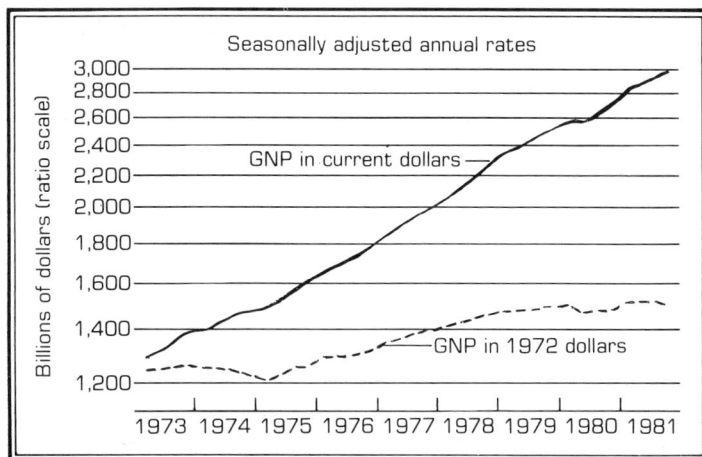

Source:  *Economic Indicators.*

Still another method of making comparisons is shown in Figure 1-2. This is a bar graph. The bar, or column, for each nation shows the relative size of per capita (per person) Gross Domestic Product (GDP) in those nations. In this illustration the dollar amounts are indicated above the individual bars. In some bar graphs the absolute dollar amounts are indicated by comparing bar heights to a vertical scale at the left, such as was used in the previous graph.

Figure 1-2.  Per capita Gross Domestic Product for selected countries (in U.S. dollars)

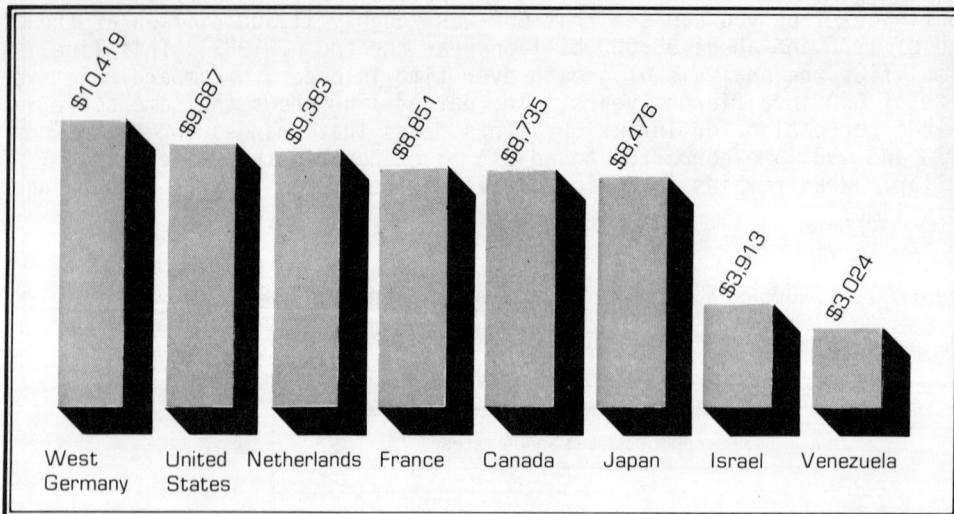

| West Germany | United States | Netherlands | France | Canada | Japan | Israel | Venezuela |
| $10,419 | $9,687 | $9,383 | $8,851 | $8,735 | $8,476 | $3,913 | $3,024 |

Source:  Prepared from *Statistical Yearbook*, 1980.  Copyright © by the United Nations.

Figure 2-3 uses a graph with no time dimension.  It differs from Figure 1-1 in that respect.  It uses vertical and horizontal scales to show how quantity demanded (left graph) and quantity supplied (right graph) change in relationship to price changes (vertical scale).  On the left, the line $D_0$ indicates one set of price-quantity relationships. The other two lines show two other sets of such relationships.  If various market conditions change, the demand line (or curve) might shift from $D_0$ to $D_1$ or $D_2$.  The graph on the right is the same except that the quantity supplied is shown on the horizontal axis.  The line $S_0$ shows a set of relationships between prices and quantities supplied at those prices.  Lines $S_1$ and $S_2$ represent different sets of such relationships. In line $S_2$ higher prices are required to elicit the same amounts to be supplied under conditions found in $S_0$ or $S_1$.

Figure 2-3.  Changes (or shifts) in demand and supply curves

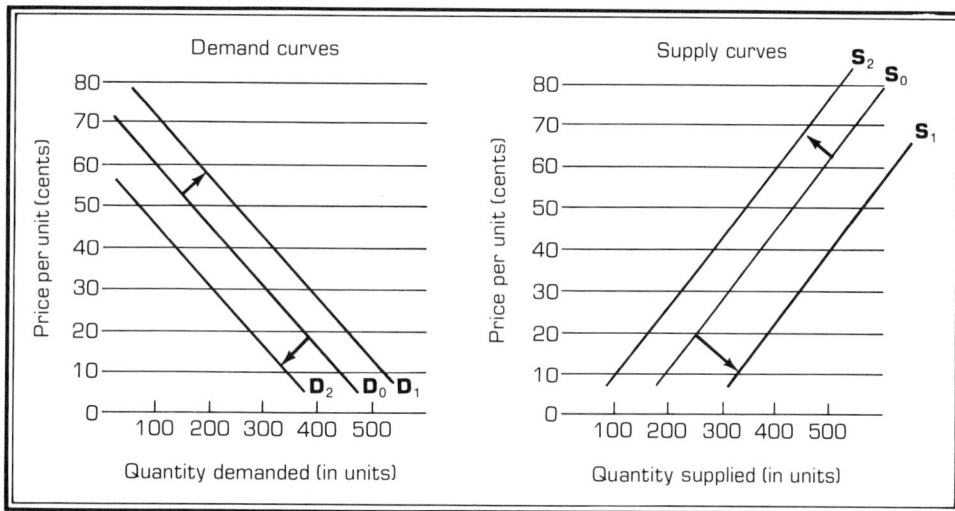

Figure 3-5 makes use of a device known as a "pie chart."  In this case a whole (100 percent) of a quantity is represented by a circle or diagram of a pie.  For example, in the pie chart on the left in Figure 3-5, the quantity is the number of firms in the United States. The slices of the pie indicate the percentage of the total that is made up of a particular category.  For example, corporations comprise about 15 out of every 100 firms, and roughly 77 out of one hundred are sole proprietorships.

Figure 4-4 is a simple continuum.  It illustrates a wide range of leadership behavior between the extremes of boss-centered leadership and subordinate-centered leadership.

Figure 3-5.  Percentages of American business firms by form of ownership and relative percentage distribution of sales revenues and net profit.

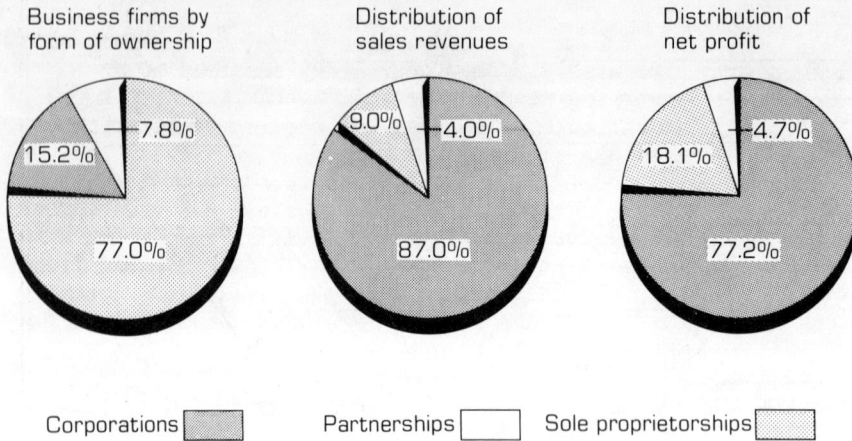

Business firms by
form of ownership

7.8%
15.2%
77.0%

Distribution of
sales revenues

9.0%  4.0%
87.0%

Distribution of
net profit

4.7%
18.1%
77.2%

Corporations          Partnerships          Sole proprietorships

Source:  *Statistical Abstract of the United States.*

Figure 4-4.  Continuum of leadership behavior

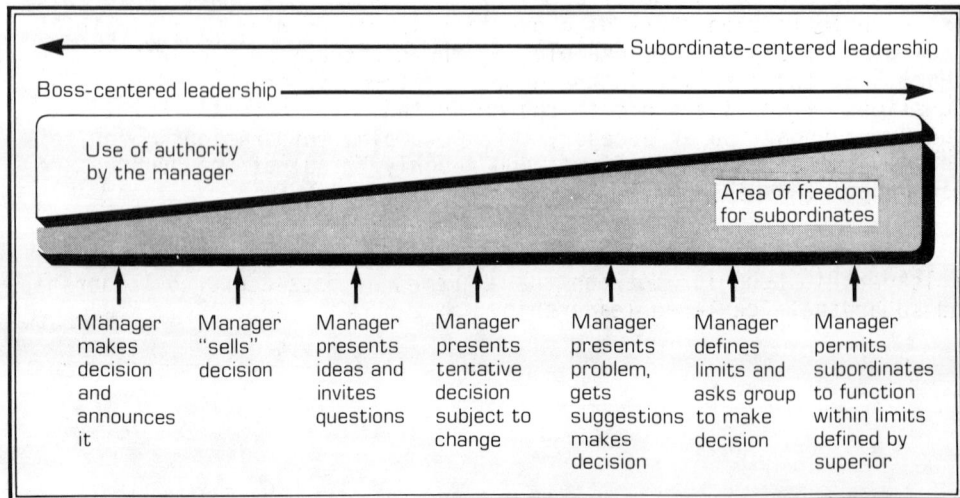

Subordinate-centered leadership

Boss-centered leadership

Use of authority
by the manager

Area of freedom
for subordinates

| Manager makes decision and announces it | Manager "sells" decision | Manager presents ideas and invites questions | Manager presents tentative decision subject to change | Manager presents problem, gets suggestions makes decision | Manager defines limits and asks group to make decision | Manager permits subordinates to function within limits defined by superior |

Source:  Robert Tannenbaum and Warren H. Schmidt, "How to Choose a Leadership Pattern," *Harvard Business Review*, May-June 1973, Exhibit 1, p. 164.  Copyright  1973 by the President and Fellows of Harvard College; all rights reserved.  Reprinted by permission of the *Harvard Business Review*.

# SOME HINTS FOR STUDYING

Your instructor will give your guidelines regarding how to study for this course. There are, however, several rather general suggestions to consider.

1. Budget your time wisely. Keep your study sessions at a reasonable length and devote your full mental capacity to them. Regular attendance in class and regular preparation for class are essential.
2. Set goals for yourself. Do not begin a course with the attitude that a "C" is the best you can earn. Consider all the reasons that exist to make the most of your ability.
3. Start with the right attitude and you will discover that the course covers things that really have meaning to you right now. For example, Chapter 5 will give you a clear understanding of the meaning of an organization, and that is useful to you now because you do belong to organizations--church, social, campus, and so forth. The course also covers things that will become increasingly important to you in the future. For example, you will develop a sharper picture of the nature of careers in business. This will definitely assist you in making career choices.
4. Get into the habit of taking notes while reading and during class meetings. Do not try to write down everything you read or everything your instructor says. Jot down the things that are most important, that is, the key words that will help you to recall what you read or heard. Develop your note-taking skill. Sum up important points in as few words as possible. Use abbreviations, short phrases, and your own version of shorthand. If you get the basic ideas presented in lectures in class, you can expand on the notes out of class. You will be amazed at how much you will be able to recall on the basis of a good lecture outline. By all means, keep your notes organized for study purposes.
5. Always read the assigned material *before* you go to class and, if possible, outline that material. This familiarizes you with the material that will be covered and helps you to take better notes in class. Do not fall into the habit of putting off your assigned reading until the day before exams. You lose in at least two ways--you do not get as much out of class lectures and discussion and you always find yourself trying to catch up.
6. Reread the chapter after class to reenforce learning.
7. If you have questions, ask them. Depending on class size and format, questions can be asked during regular class sessions, discussion sessions, or your instructor's office hours.
8. Prepare your assignments on time. Late work is usually penalized when graded.
9. A good policy to follow is to assume that a quiz will be given at each class meeting. This tends to encourage you to keep

up with your assignments.

10. Informal discussion among students can be a very helpful learning experience. You can share your ideas and opinions with other students outside of class.

11. Keep informed about what is happening in the business world. Business is constantly changing. Your library probably subscribes to *The Wall Street Journal, Business Week, Fortune, The Harvard Business Review,* and other newspapers, magazines, and journals. Set time aside to browse through one or more of these on a regular basis. The topics discussed in your text deal with the business world. You can find articles in journals and newspapers, for example, that deal with what business is doing about social problems. You also can find articles that discuss what particular companies are doing to correct those problems. Of course, there are also many articles that discuss management, production, marketing, finance, accounting, computers, etc. Find examples of what business firms are doing in some of these areas. This can help in stimulating class discussion. By reading current articles, you are putting forth that extra effort that helps you to keep up-to-date on developments in business.

12. Keep an open mind. Be willing to consider and evaluate new ideas. Business is dynamic. A closed mind can be a very costly thing to a student of business.

STUDY GUIDE FOR
# INTRODUCTION TO BUSINESS

# CHAPTER 1

# Approaching the Economic Problem

Chapter 1 provides an overview of our economic system. Given the economic problem of attempting to satisfy unlimited wants with limited resources, economic systems, such as capitalism and collectivism, evolve to provide a framework for need satisfaction. No two economic systems will approach problems in an identical manner. For example, capitalism emphasizes individualism, private property, and profit incentive. In purely collectivist economic systems, economic goals are reached through central planning. There is no private property and no recognition of profit.

The task of satisfying wants is more complicated today than in earlier years because of the increased diversity of wants. This diversity makes the measurement of an economy's performance more difficult. Some specific measures of performance include Gross National Product and Disposable Personal Income.

In addition to discussing the economic problem, this chapter describes several basic concepts (utility, value, specialization, exchange, factors of production, and diminishing marginal utility) that are applicable to any type of economic system. These concepts provide a fundamental understanding of the basic building blocks of our economic system.

The chapter ends with a brief introduction to the nature of business. In our economic system business is all profit-directed economic activities that are organized and directed to provide goods and services. Profit is considered the key motivator of business activities in our economic system.

# TEST YOUR BUSINESS VOCABULARY

Test your business vocabulary by matching each key concept with the appropriate phrase. Check your answers with those at the end of this chapter.

## Key Concepts

___ 1. capital formation
___ 2. capitalism
___ 3. central planning
___ 4. consumerism
___ 5. Disposable Personal Income (DPI)
___ 6. entrepreneurship
___ 7. exchange
___ 8. factors of production
___ 9. Gross National Product (GNP)
___ 10. laissez faire
___ 11. Protestant ethic
___ 12. specialization
___ 13. standard of living
___ 14. the economic problem
___ 15. utility
___ 16. collectivism

## Phrases

A. Concentrating more effort on a specific task instead of dividing one's efforts among a greater number of tasks
B. The capacity of a product or service to satisfy a human want
C. Land, labor, capital, and entrepreneurship
D. The amount of money a family has left over after buying basic necessities
E. Key concern or all nations, individuals, businesses, and other oganizations
F. Giving up one thing to get another thing
G. This is used to compare the well-being of one society with that of another society and to observe change in well-being over time
H. Some of the major features of this economic system are individualism, private property, and profit incentive
I. Government ownership of the factors of production and government control of all economic activities
J. A philosophy that emphasizes the value of hard work, accumulation of property, and self-reliance
K. The incomes of people minus taxes paid by them
L. All profit-directed economic activities that are organized and directed to provide goods and services
M. The market value of all final goods and services produced by a nation during a given year
N. The owners of business set the rules of competition without any government regulation or control
O. The ability of one product or service to command another product or service in an exchange
P. Occurs when a person or firm assumes risk in the hope of making a profit
Q. The concept that the consumer influences the quality, style, etc. of products produced by business firms and determines the success of those firms

2

R. An approach in which the government drafts a master plan of what it wants to accomplish and directly manages the economy to achieve the plan's goals

S. A movement to enhance the power of consumers relative to that of business firms

T. The process of adding to the productive capacity of an economy

## PROGRAMMED REVIEW

(To help you in understanding the chapter material and to see if you have mastered the objectives stated at the beginning of the chapter)

1. *Define the economic problem and discuss how we cope with it.*

   A. The economic problem is _____

   _____

   _____

   B. _____ (concentrating on a particular task) and _____ (giving up one thing to get another thing) are ways of coping with the economic problem.

2. *Describe ways in which the performance of an economic system is measured.*

   Define the following types of indicators of an economy's performance.

   A. standard of living:_____

   _____

   B. Gross National Product (GNP):_____

   _____

   C. inflation: _____

   _____

   D. Disposable Personal Income (DPI):_____

   _____

3. *Define utility and explain the concept of value in exchange.*

   A. Utility means _____ in satisfying wants.

   B. A commodity that is extremely plentiful, such as air, will have value in _____ but no value in _____.

   C. Something has _____ when it can command something else in return for it.

4. *List and define the factors of production.*

   A. The four factors of production are _____, _____, _____, and _____.

   B. Define and give examples of each factor of production.

   _____

   _____

   _____

   _____

   _____

5. *State the basic purpose of an economic system and give examples of economic systems that reflect this basic purpose.*

   A. The purpose of an economic system is to provide a _____ for _____ human _____ and _____.

   B. Define mercantilism:_____

   _____

   C. Define laissez faire:_____

   _____

6. *Compare and contrast the collectivist and capitalist economic systems.*

4

A. Capitalism is an economic system based on _____ ownership of the _____ of production.

B. _____ _____, which means that the government drafts a master plan for the economy, is a key element in a collectivist economic system.

7. *List and discuss the chief characteristics of a capitalist economic system.*

A. individualism _____

_____

B. private property _____

_____

C. profit incentive _____

_____

D. consumer power _____

_____

E. freedom to compete _____

_____

F. occupational freedom _____

_____

G. freedom of contract _____

_____

H. limited role of government _____

_____

8. *Explain why real-world economic systems are not pure and give examples.*

A. Briefly explain why the economic system in the United States is not the pure ideal of capitalism.

_____

_____

5

B. Briefly explain why collectivism in some countries is not the pure ideal of collectivism.

_____

_____

9. *Define business and discuss the role of profit in business activity.*

A. Business is all _____-directed economic activities that are organized and directed to provide goods and services.

B. Profit is _____

_____

10. *Describe a postindustrial economy.*

A. A postindustrial economy is based on the creation of _____ services.

B. Give some examples of services.

_____

_____

TEST YOURSELF (Multiple Choice)

Test yourself by selecting the best answer. Check your answers with those at the end of this chapter.

1. Economic systems help us to do all of the following, except:

   A. cope with the economic problem
   B. satisfy our wants
   C. use our scarce resources better
   D. provide the means for individuals to become totally self-sufficient

2. Which of the following factors of production is associated with the human mental and physical effort needed to produce goods and services?

   A. land
   B. labor
   C. capital
   D. entrepreneurship

3. Which of the following is <u>not</u> a characteristic of a collectivist economic system?

    A. profit incentive
    B. central planning
    C. little freedom of contract
    D. the belief that competition results in economic waste

4. In order for a good or service to have any utility, it must:

    A. be readily available
    B. have a money price attached to it
    C. be capable of satisfying a certain want
    D. be desired by all individuals

5. Specialization means that a person:

    A. gives less effort to fewer tasks
    B. gives more effort to a specific task
    C. gives less effort to a greater number of tasks
    D. gives more effort to a greater number of tasks

6. Gross National Product (GNP) is:

    A. the sum of the market values of all final goods and services produced by a nation during a given year
    B. a smaller figure than Disposable Personal Income (DPI)
    C. the same for all industrialized nations
    D. a good measure of the quality of life in a nation

7. According to capitalist theory, competition among firms is:

    A. good for consumers but bad for firms
    B. good for firms but bad for consumers
    C. good for consumers and firms
    D. bad for consumers and firms

8. Consumer power is:

    A. the freedom each person has to choose his or her own occupation
    B. the freedom that consumers have to buy from whomever they choose
    C. the freedom to take a risk in the hope of profit
    D. limited by government interference in our personal lives

9. Mercantilism:

    A. emphasized the importance of reducing export trade
    B. had as its goal to increase the government's holdings of precious metals such as gold and silver

C. means the same as laissez faire
D. was not an economic philosophy

10. People in capitalist economies go into business and take on risk mainly because:

A. consumer power exists
B. this assures them of making a profit
C. they believe in central planning
D. the profit incentive is present

TEST YOURSELF (TRUE-FALSE)

Test yourself by answering whether the following statements are true or false. Check your answers with those at the end of this chapter.

____ 1. The process of exchange organizes people into groups and an economic system is the result.

____ 2. Utility is one of the most important factors of production.

____ 3. Entrepreneurship is one of the most important factors of production.

____ 4. The Protestant ethic is a philosophy that argues against material progress.

____ 5. A postindustrial economy is based on the creation of intangible services.

____ 6. Capital formation is the process of adding to the productive capacity of an economy.

____ 7. The principle of diminishing marginal utility basically states that the more you have of an item, the more you want (and the more you are willing to pay) to get more of the item.

____ 8. Capital, as a factor of production, means human-made productive capacity.

____ 9. Within the context of a capitalistic economic system, the right of private property is related to individualism.

____ 10. Capitalism is the only economic system in which human wants are unlimited while the resources with which to satisfy them are limited.

EXERCISE 1-1

(To help you to understand the differences between capitalism and collectivism)

Indicate with an X whether the characteristics listed on the left are more closely associated with capitalism or with collectivism.

|  | Capitalism | Collectivism |
|---|---|---|
| 1. central planning determines how resources will be used | | |
| 2. profit incentive | | |
| 3. freedom of contract | | |
| 4. little or no private property | | |
| 5. the government drafts a master plan of what it wants to accomplish and directly manages the economy to achieve the plan's goals | | |
| 6. individual consumers make independent choices by exercising their consumer power | | |
| 7. wage rates and prices of products are set by the government | | |
| 8. an egalitarian system | | |
| 9. right of private property | | |
| 10. freedom to compete | | |

EXERCISE 1-2

(To help you to understand the nature of the economic problem)

1.  What are the reasons for the existence of the economic problem?

2.  Is the economic problem applicable to business firms, nonprofit
    organizations, and individuals?  Explain and give examples.

3.  Discuss the importance of specialization and exchange in our
    economic system.

4.  Given the economic problem will continue to plague us, how can we
    better cope with it?

EXERCISE 1-3

(To involve yourself in contemporary business)

Interview a business owner in your community and write down his or her answers to the following questions:

1.  What product(s) and/or service(s) do you offer for sale?

2.  Why did you go into business for yourself?

3.  In your own words, what is profit?

4.  In your opinion, what is the most important factor affecting the profitability of your business?

EXERCISE 1-4

(Crossword Puzzle Review)

Across

2. A measure of economic well-being (3 words)
4. The incomes of people minus taxes paid by them (abbreviation
5. Means trade
8. The inputs of the productive system (3 words)
10. Protestant _____(s)
11. Precious metals in the state treasury
12. Sum
13. The ability of one product or service to command another product or service (3 words)

Down

1. An economic system in which the factors of production are privately owned
3. Dividing work into several tasks and having one person perform only a limited number of those tasks
5. Land, labor, capital, and

_____
6. The market value of all final goods and services produced by a country during a year (abbreviation)
7. Practiced in collectivist economic systems (2 words)

12

Across

15. Means "hands off" (2 words)
16. Process of adding to an
    economy's productive capacity
    (2 words)

Down

9. The factors of production are
   owned by the government

12. Sum
14. Usefulness

EXERCISE 1-5

(Incident: Used-car Dealers)

Answer the questions on a plain piece of paper.


The Federal Trade Commission (FTC) was created in 1914 to help protect consumers. In 1975 Congress ordered the FTC to issue a rule covering sales of used cars by dealers. Congress issued the order because of widespread consumer complaints about used-car dealers.

After having conducted an intensive investigation of the used-car business, the FTC issued a rule in 1982 that required used-car dealers to disclose known major defects in the cars they offer for sale. Each car would have a window sticker which disclosed the defects. Also, the sticker would indicate whether the dealer provided a warranty on the car or was offering it for sale "as is".

The FTC's rule, however, did not go into effect. A 1980 law allows Congress to veto FTC regulations and, in May 1982, the used-car rule was vetoed by Congress. Opponents of the rule argued it would result in higher prices for used cars because the dealers would pass on the cost of auto inspections to consumers. Proponents of the rule argued that consumers needed protection and that Congress should not have veto power over FTC regulations.

Questions

1. Discuss the concept of the utility of a used car to its former owner and a prospective buyer of that used car.
2. Is the concept of laissez faire applicable to the Congressional veto of the FTC's used-car rule? Explain.
3. Do you think consumerism played a role in the FTC's decision to issue the used-car rule? Why or why not?
4. If the FTC's rule had gone into effect, would it have limited freedom of contract between used-car dealers and their prospective customers? Discuss.
5. Suppose you had been a member of Congress in May 1982. Would you have voted to veto the FTC's used-car rule? Why or why not?

# CHAPTER 1 ANSWERS

Test Your Business
Vocabulary

| | |
|---|---|
| 1. T (p. 20) | 9. M (p. 9) |
| 2. H (p. 16) | 10. N (p. 15) |
| 3. R (p. 17) | 11. J (p. 17) |
| 4. S (p. 20) | 12. A (p. 5) |
| 5. K (p. 11) | 13. G (p. 9) |
| 6. P (P. 14) | 14. E (p. 4) |
| 7. F (p. 7) | 15. B (p. 11) |
| 8. C (p. 12) | 16. I (p. 16) |

Programmed Review
(refer to the indicated pages
in the text)

1.
  A. (p. 4)
  B. (pp. 5,7)
2.
  A. (p. 9)
  B. (p. 9)
  C. (p. 9)
  D. (p. 10)
3.
  A. (p. 11)
  B. (p. 11)
  C. (p. 11)
4.
  A. (p. 12)
  B. (pp. 12-14)
5.
  A. (p. 15)
  B. (p. 15)
  C. (p. 15)

6.
  A. (p. 16)
  B. (p. 17)
7.
  A. (p. 17)
  B. (pp. 18-19)
  C. (pp. 19-20)
  D. (pp. 20-21)
  E. (p. 21)
  F. (pp. 21-22)
  G. (p. 22)
  H. (pp. 22-23)
8.
  A. (pp. 25-26)
  B. (p. 24)
9.
  A. (p. 27)
  B. (p. 27)
10.
  A. (p. 27)
  B. (p. 28)

Exercise 1-1

Capitalism:
  2 (p. 19), 3 (p. 22), 6 (p. 20),
  9 (p. 18), 10 (p. 21)
Collectivism:
  1 (p. 17), 4 (p. 23), 5 (p. 17),
  7 (p. 24), 8 (p. 17)

Exercise 1-4

Down:
  1. capitalism (p. 16)
  3. specialization (p. 5)
  5. entrepreneurship (p. 12)
  6. GNP (p. 9)
  7. central planning (p. 17)
  9. collectivism (p. 16)
14. utility (p. 11)

Across:
  2. standard of living (p. 9)
  4. DPI (p. 10)
  5. exchange (p. 7)
  8. factors of production (p. 12)
10. ethic(s) (p. 17)
11. mercantilism (p. 15)
12. total (no page reference)
13. value in exchange (p. 11)
15. laissez faire (p. 15)
16. capital formation (p. 20)

Test Yourself (Multiple Choice)

| | |
|---|---|
| 1. D (p. 4) | 6. A (p. 9) |
| 2. B (p. 13) | 7. C (p. 21) |
| 3. A (p. 23) | 8. B (p. 20) |
| 4. C (p. 11) | 9. B (p. 15) |
| 5. B (p. 5) | 10. D (p. 19) |

Test Yourself (True-False)

| | |
|---|---|
| 1. True (p. 7) | 6. True (p. 20) |
| 2. False (p. 12) | 7. False (p. 12) |
| 3. True (p. 14) | 8. True (p. 14) |
| 4. False (p. 17) | 9. True (p. 18) |
| 5. True (p. 27) | 10. False (p. 3) |

# The Market Economy and the Business Firm

This chapter introduces the concept of the market economy and the role it plays in satisfying needs and wants. A market economy exists when prices are used to determine the manner in which resources are allocated.

Before prices are determined, both demand and supply must exist. Demand for a good or service occurs when there are people who desire the good or service, have the buying power to purchase it, and are willing to part with some buying power to purchase it. The demand for goods and services may be influenced by such factors as buying power, population changes, and changes in tastes and cultural values. Supply results from the efforts of producers. Some factors affecting supply are competition, economic outlook, and a firm's objectives.

After presenting the specifics of supply and demand, the chapter focuses on price determination. Price, the cornerstone of a market economy, is determined at the point where the demand curve intersects the supply curve. This is the equilibrium price because buyers can buy all that they are willing to and sellers can supply all they desire.

Chapter 2 ends with an analysis of why firms enter into business. The key motivator is profit. In addition to profit, some people feel that business firms should pursue social responsibility as a goal.

# TEST YOUR BUSINESS VOCABULARY

Test your business vocabulary by matching each key concept with the appropriate phrase. Check your answers with those at the end of this chapter.

## Key Concepts

____ 1. market economy
____ 2. demand
____ 3. law of demand
____ 4. supply
____ 5. law of supply
____ 6. risk
____ 7. real income

____ 8. business opportunity
____ 9. price
____ 10. discretionary income
____ 11. demand curve
____ 12. supply curve

## Phrases

A. A set of economic forces which together form a price
B. An economic system in which prices determine how resources will be allocated and how the goods and services produced will be distributed
C. The amount of money (or other goods and services) that is paid in exchange for something else
D. The desire on the part of a would-be buyer
E. What remains of your disposable income after you have bought your necessities
F. That income remaining after taxes
G. Income expressed in terms of buying power
H. The demand for all goods and services in an economy
I. Exists when there are people who desire a good or service, they have the buying power to purchase it, and a willingness to buy it
J. A line that shows the number of units that will be bought at each price at a given point in time
K. The chance of loss
L. At this point the demand curve intersects the supply curve
M. A set of circumstances that may enable a person or firm to reap some benefit or profit
N. More of a good or service is demanded at a lower price than at a higher price
O. A line that shows the number of units that will be offered for sale at each price at a given point in time
P. The quantity of a good or a service that is made available for sale as the result of effort by producers
Q. More of a good or service is offered for sale at a higher price than at a lower price
R. Tax cuts would leave consumers with more money to spend and business people with more money to invest

PROGRAMMED REVIEW

(To help you in understanding the chapter material and to see if you
have mastered the objectives stated at the beginning of the chapter)

1. *Explain what a market economy is and how it works.*

    A.  A. market economy is an _____ system in which _____

        determine how resources will be allocated.

    B.  _____ and _____ interact to form a price.

2. *Define the law of demand and explain why it is valid.*

    A.  The _____ relationship between _____ and quantity

        demanded is the law of demand.

    B.  For most products a greater number of units are demanded at a
        lower price.  One reason for this is the principle of _____

        _____.

3. *Identify and describe the major factors that influence the overall
   demand for goods and services in an economy.*

    A.  The six major nonprice factors underlying demand are _____

        _____ , _____ ,

        _____ , _____ ,

        _____ , and _____ .

    B.  Buying power comes from _____ , _____

        _____ , and _____ .

4. *Define the law of supply and explain why it is valid.*

    A.  The law of supply states _____

        _____ .

    B.  Why will higher prices lead producers to supply more units than

        a lower price?_____ .

5. *Explain the major factors that influence the overall supply of
   goods and services in an economy.*

The eight major factors that influence supply are: _____

_____, _____,

_____, _____,

_____, _____,

_____, and _____.

6. *Draw a demand curve and a supply curve and explain the significance of their intersection on a graph.*

   A.  A demand curve is _____

   _____

   B.  A supply curve is _____

   _____

   C.  _____ is determined at the intersection of supply and

   demand.

7. *Distinguish between a change in demand and a change in quantity demanded.*

   A.  A change in quantity demanded means that a greater or lesser number of units is bought because of a change in _____.

   B.  A change in demand means _____

   _____.

8. *Distinguish between a change in supply and a change in quantity supplied.*

   A.  A change in supply means _____

   _____.

   B.  A change in quantity supplied means _____

   _____.

9. *Discuss the importance of profit opportunity to business firms.*

   A.  If a firm's sales revenues and costs are equal, it earns no

   profit, but it does _____ _____.

B.  A business opportunity _____

_____

_____

10. *Explain why business owners assume risk.*

A.  Risk is defined as _____.

B.  The hope of _____ explains risk-assumption.

TEST YOURSELF (Multiple Choice)

Test yourself by selecting the best answer.  Check your answers with
those at the end of this chapter.

1.  A change in the quantity demanded of a good or service is most
    likely to be caused by which one of the following?

    A.  changes in buying power
    B.  changes in tastes and cultural values
    C.  changes in prices
    D.  population shifts

2.  The point at which the demand and supply curves for a given good
    cross indicates:

    A.  the equilibrium price
    B.  that demand is greater than supply
    C.  that supply is greater than demand
    D.  that the demand curve has shifted

3.  Which of the following is not a requirement for the existence of
    demand for a good or service?

    A.  perfect information
    B.  desire for it
    C.  buying power to purchase it
    D.  a willingness to part with some of the buying power to buy it

4.  A person who assumes risk is indicating that:

    A.  he or she considers the chance of loss greater than the poten-
        tial reward
    B.  the expected profit is worth the risk involved
    C.  any investor would leap at the investment opportunity
    D.  there is an assurance of gain

5. The law of supply tells us that:

   A. the supply of a given good is not related to its price
   B. as the price of a given good goes up, the quantity supplied goes down
   C. as the price of a given good goes up, the quantity supplied goes up
   D. as the price of a given good changes, there is a shift in the supply curve.

6. Which of the following phrases best describes a market economy?

   A. an economic system in which the government determines how resources will be allocated
   B. an economic system in which prices determine how resources will be allocated
   C. an economic system that utilizes a very sophisticated approach to barter
   D. an economic system that de-emphasizes the forces of supply and demand

7. When a greater or a lesser number of units of a product is supplied because of a change in price, a _____ has occurred.

   A. change in demand
   B. change in supply
   C. change in quantity demanded
   D. change in quantity supplied

8. Which of the following is the major source of buying power?

   A. accumulated wealth
   B. current income
   C. installment credit
   D. noninstallment credit

9. Of the factors that influence supply, which of the following is most closely associated with tax incentives?

   A. nature of competition
   B. technological progress
   C. outlook for the economy
   D. government spending policies and regulations

10. The key motivation for most business firms is:

   A. profit
   B. risk
   C. opportunity
   D. specialization and exchange

TEST YOURSELF (True-False)

Test yourself by answering whether the following statements are true or false.  Check your answers with those at the end of this chapter.

____  1.  Prices induce or limit production and consumption.

____  2.  In a market economy, the choice of which goods and services will be produced is made by a centralized government planning agency.

____  3.  The most important factor influencing a change in the quantity demanded of a good or service is changes in tastes and cultural values.

____  4.  According to the law of supply, as price goes up, the quantity supplied goes up.

____  5.  A typical demand curve slopes down and to the right.

____  6.  According to the Keynesian school of economic thought, inflation can be reduced by using tax increases to reduce demand.

____  7.  Whenever the quantity demanded of a good or service is greater than the quantity supplied, a surplus condition exists.

____  8.  Business activity involves gathering and allocating resources in the hope of profit.

____  9.  Liquid wealth cannot be converted quickly into a known amount of cash for making purchases.

____ 10.  A change in demand means that a greater or lesser number of units of a product is bought without changing price.

EXERCISE 2-1

(To help you understand the law of demand and the law of supply)

1.  State the law of demand.

2.  Construct a graph on which you illustrate the law of demand. Label
    the graph with price and quantity.

3.  State the law of supply.

4.  Construct a graph on which you illustrate the law of supply. Label
    the graph with price and quantity.

EXERCISE 2-2

(To enhance your understanding of buying power)

1. Define the following and provide an example of each one:

    a.  current income

    b.  disposable income

    c.  discretionary income

    d.  real income

    e.  liquid wealth

    f.  nonliquid wealth

    g.  installment credit

    h.  noninstallment credit

2. How does inflationary psychology affect the willingness of consumers to spend?

EXERCISE 2-3

(To help you understand the nature of business activity)

Unscramble the following list of words and phrases and place them in the appropriate spaces below.  The correct placement of the words or phrases will create a set of statements that summarizes the nature of business activity.

| | |
|---|---|
| Marketing activity | Markets |
| Decision making | Land |
| Profit | Marketable goods and services |
| Markets | Labor |
| Specialization and exchange | Risk |
| Entrepreneurship | Profit |
| Opportunity | Factors of production |
| Effort | Capital |
| Prices | Price system |
| Entrepreneurship | Production activity |
| Demand | Costs |
| Risk Assumption | Price system |
| Supply | Choice process |

### The Nature of Business Activity

_____ is exerted to exploit _____

_____ is created to satisfy _____

_____ are determined in _____

_____ is concerned with _____

_____ is assumed in the _____
                            hope of
_____ involves a recognition of _____

_____ is necessary because of the _____

_____ is guided by the _____

_____ are made productive through _____

_____ are converted to _____

_____ is guided by the _____

_____ exist because of _____

25

EXERCISE 2-4

(Crossword Puzzle Review)

Across

2. Exists when circumstances enable one who exploits it to profit
5. An economy where prices are determined through interaction of supply and demand
7. The chance of loss
8. Applies to supply and demand; graphically, becomes the supply curve or the demand curve

Down

1. Why business firms gather and organize resources for production
3. The amount of a good people will buy at a certain price
4. The quantity of money (or anything else) paid in exchange for something
6. In connection with demand, slopes down and to the right; in connection with supply, slopes up and to the right
8. The amount of a product sellers are willing to offer for sale at a certain price

EXERCISE 2-5

(Incident: An Oil Glut)

Answer the following questions on a plain piece of paper.

The price of oil skyrocketed in the years following the 1973-1974 Arab oil embargo. Members of the Organization of Petroleum Exporting Countries (OPEC) were in a position to dictate oil prices because OPEC was the major oil supplier in the world. Representatives from each member country met periodically to set the price they would charge for their oil.

But by late 1981, the demand for oil decreased because of worldwide recession and energy conservation measures. Because this occurred in the face of steady output by OPEC, oil prices started to decline. The issue came to a head in March, 1982, when representatives of OPEC met to agree on production quotas. Each member nation agreed to reduce its daily output by an agreed-upon percentage in the hope of drying up what had become an oil glut.

Questions

1. In Chapter 2 of the text, we said that "prices induce or limit production and consumption." Explain how the above developments relate to that statement.

2. How did the skyrocketing price of oil immediately after the embargo affect the lifestyle of the typical consumer in the United States?

3. Explain how energy conservation and recession could cause a decrease in demand for oil.

4. Do OPEC's actions interfere with the forces of supply and demand? Explain.

Test Your Business
Vocabulary

1. B (p. 34)        7. G (p. 56)
2. I (p. 36)        8. M (p. 56)
3. N (pp. 36-37)    9. C (p. 35)
4. P (p. 43)       10. E (pp. 37-38)
5. Q (p. 43)       11. J (p. 47)
6. K (p. 57)       12. O (p. 47)

Programmed Review
(refer to the indicated pages
in the text)

1.                  6.
    A. (p. 34)          A. (p. 47)
    B. (p. 34)          B. (p. 47)
2.                      C. (p. 47)
    A. (p. 36)      7.
    B. (p. 36)          A. (pp. 49-50)
3.                      B. (pp. 49-50)
    A. (pp. 36-37)  8.
    B. (p. 37)          A. (pp. 49-50)
4.                      B. (pp. 49-50)
    A. (p. 43)      9.
    B. (p. 43)          A. (pp. 52-53)
5.                      B. (p. 56)
    (p. 43)        10.
                        A. (p. 57)
                        B. (p. 57)

Exercise 2-2

1. a - h (pp. 37-39)
2. (p. 39)

Exercise 2-4

Down:

1. profit
3. demand
4. price
6. curve
8. supply

Across:

2. opportunity
5. market economy
7. risk
9. law

Test Yourself (Multiple Choice)

1. C (p. 49)
2. A (pp. 47-48)
3. A (p. 36)
4. B (pp. 56-58)
5. C (p. 43)
6. B (p. 34)
7. D (pp. 49-50)
8. B (p. 37)
9. D (p. 46)
10. A (p. 52)

Test Yourself (True-False)

1. True (p. 34)
2. False (p. 34)
3. False (p. 36)
4. True (p. 43)
5. True (pp. 47-49)
6. True (p. 44)
7. False (pp. 47-48)
8. True (p. 52)
9. False (p. 39)
10. True (pp. 49-50)

# CHAPTER 3

# Forms of Business Ownership

Chapter 3 is designed to acquaint you with the various forms of business ownership. The different forms of ownership show alternative ways fo pursuing the profit motive. The three dominant types of ownership are the sole proprietorship, partnership, and corporation.

A sole proprietorship is a business owned and managed by one person. The key advantages are simplicity in starting the business, ownership of all the profits, and the personal satisfaction derived from owning your business. However, accompanying these advantages are the problems of unlimited financial liability for business debts and the impermanence of the business firm.

Partnerships have the advantages of greater borrowing power and more opportunity for specialization. Partnerships share the same basic disadvantages with sole proprietorships, with the addition of potential for personal disagreements between partners.

The corporate form was created to overcome some of the problems associated with sole proprietorships and partnerships. Some of the basic strengths of this method of organization are limited financial capability, and its existence as a separate legal entity. The major drawbacks of this form are special and double taxation and complicated and costly formation.

The chapter ends with a discussion of other forms of ownership, such as limited partnerships, joint ventures, business trusts, cooperative associations, and mutual companies. All of these forms provide alternatives to persons considering going into business. Each one must be carefully evaluated in terms of advantages and disadvantages, and must be consistent with the nature of the business activity to be pursued.

# TEST YOUR BUSINESS VOCABULARY

Test your business vocabulary by matching each key concept with the proper phrase.  Check your answers with those at the end of this chapter.

## Key Concepts

____ 1. unlimited liability
____ 2. corporation
____ 3. stockholders
____ 4. professional managers
____ 5. common stockholders
____ 6. preferred stockholders
____ 7. countervailing power
____ 8. joint venture
____ 9. sole proprietorship
____ 10. partnership
____ 11. mutual company
____ 12. corporate charter
____ 13. board of directors
____ 14. proxy
____ 15. Subchapter S Corporation

## Phrases

A. An individual who is appointed to represent another individual
B. A document indicating the rules by which the corporation will operate
C. They are the residual owners of a corporation
D. A business arrangement, created by an agreement, in which a trustee holds the property, runs the business, and accepts funds from investors
E. The group of persons, elected by a corporation's stockholders, that is ultimately responsible for the management of that corporation
F. This form of business ownership involves a group of persons who act together to accomplish some purpose, but it does not seek to earn a profit in the usual sense of the term
G. These stockholders usually do not have the right to vote
H. A small corporation with no more than 25 stockholders that can choose to be taxed as a partnership and still enjoy the advantages of incorporation
I. Liability extends to their personal property and, possibly real property
J. The firm and the owner are the same
K. A contract between the owners of a partnership
L. An association of two or more persons to carry on as co-owners of a business for profit
M. An example is a life insurance company that is owned by its policyholders
N. A separate and legal entity apart from its owners
O. A special type of temporary partnership arrangement that is set up for a specific purpose and ends when that purpose is accomplished
P. The owners of the entity that is the corporation
Q. Most often used when there is a separation of ownership and management in a firm
R. This term describes the balance of influence between labor, business, and government

S.  It authorizes the formation of a corporation
T.  Requires agreement and consideration


PROGRAMMED REVIEW

(To help you in understanding the chapter material and to see if you
have mastered the objectives stated at the beginning of the chapter)

1.  *Identify the reasons for and give examples of the growth of public
    ownership in the United States.*

    The four basic reasons why public ownership may be undertaken are:

    _____

    _____

    _____

    _____

    _____.

2.  *Identify the three most common forms of private ownership in the
    United States.*

    The three most common forms of private ownership are:_____

    _____, _____, and _____.

3.  *List and compare the relative advantages and disadvantages of the
    three major forms of ownership of business firms.*

    A.  Simplicity in starting the business; ownership of all profits,
        and simplicity in dissolving the business are advantages of the

        _____  _____.

    B.  Unlimited and joint financial liability and impermanence of the
        business firm are disadvantages of the _____.

    C.  Greater financial capability and the easy transfer of ownership
        are advantages of the _____.

    D.  Lack of secrecy in operations and special and double taxation
        are disadvantages of the _____.

4.  *Outline the basic procedures involved in forming and operating a
    corporation.*

31

A. What are some of the steps in forming a corporation? _____

_____

_____.

B. A domestic corporation is _____

_____.

C. A corporate charter is _____

_____

5. *Discuss the relative importance of the three major forms of owner-ship in terms of the number of firms, sales revenues received, and profit earned.*

A. _____ receive 87 percent of all sales revenues and 77.2 percent of all net profit of American firms.

B. _____ receive 4 percent of all sales revenues and 4.7 per-cent of all net profit of American firms.

C. _____ _____ receive 9 percent of all sales revenues and 18.1 percent of all net profit of American firms.

6. *Identify and discuss the relative advantages and disadvantages of large-scale operations.*

A. The four basic advantages of large-scale operations are _____

_____

_____

_____

_____.

B. The four basic disadvantages of large-scale operations are ____

_____

_____

_____

_____.

7. *List and discuss other forms of business ownership that are modifications of the three basic forms of ownership.*

   A.  A _____ _____ has at least one general partner and one or more limited partners.

   B.  A _____ association is a group of persons who act together to accomplish some purpose.


TEST YOURSELF (Multiple Choice)

Test yourself by selecting the best answer.  Check your answers with those at the end of this chapter.

1. Which of the following is a major disadvantage of the sole proprietorship form of ownership?

   A. limited financial liability
   B. ease of raising funds for expansion
   C. no sharing of the burden of management
   D. permanence of the business firm

2. The document that states the purpose for which a corporation is being formed is called the:

   A. corporation bylaws
   B. common stock charter
   C. partnership agreement
   D. corporate charter

3. In a corporation:

   A. the stockholders elect the corporate officers
   B. the corporate officers elect the board of directors
   C. the stockholders elect the board of directors
   D. the president appoints members to the board of directors

4. The most common form of ownership in the United States is:

   A. the sole proprietorship
   B. the partnership
   C. the corporation
   D. the mutual cooperative

5. All of the following are advantages of large-scale operations, except:

   A. greater borrowing power
   B. greater opportunity for specialization by workers and managers
   C. greater availability of managerial talent

D. greater personal contact between workers and managers

6. If you own 10 shares of common stock in a corporation that is holding an election for five board members and the law requires cumulative voting, you have:

   A. 10 votes
   B. 50 votes
   C. 5 votes
   D. 1 vote

7. A corporation's shareholders:

   A. are the corporation
   B. possess unlimited liability for corporate debts
   C. are the owners of the firm
   D. cannot participate directly in managing the firm

8. A partner who does not actively participate in managing the firm but whose name is identified with the firm is called a:

   A. secret partner
   B. silent partner
   C. dormant (sleeping) partner
   D. nominal partner

9. Employee credit unions are examples of:

   A. joint ventures
   B. limited partnerships
   C. mutual companies
   D. cooperative associations

10. Public ownership of the means of production in the United States:

   A. is more unpopular today than it was a century ago
   B. does not exist
   C. may be undertaken when the needed investment is too great for private investors
   D. is the main form of ownership

TEST YOURSELF (True-False)

Test yourself by answering whether the following statements are true or false. Check your answers with those at the end of the chapter.

____ 1. Public ownership is the main type of ownership in the United States.

34

_____ 2. One of the major problems with the sole proprietorship is the complexity of dissolving the business.

_____ 3. General partners have unlimited liability for the business debts of the partnership.

_____ 4. The corporation is a creation of government authority.

_____ 5. All public and quasi-public corporations seek to earn a profit.

_____ 6. The Subchapter S Corporation firm allows the owners to enjoy the advantages of incorporation while avoiding the disadvantages of double taxation.

_____ 7. If a corporation goes bankrupt the common stockholders are the first to receive any proceeds from the sale of the corporation's property.

_____ 8. With cumulative voting, the number of votes a stockholder has is the number of shares he or she owns times the number of directors to be elected.

_____ 9. Owner-managers manage most large American corporations.

_____ 10. A mutual company is similar to a cooperative because the users are the owners.

EXERCISE 3-1

(To review the relative advantages and disadvantages of the three most common forms of business ownership)

Place an X in the space(s) under the form(s) of ownership to which the phrase applies:

| | SOLE PROPRIETORSHIP | GENERAL PARTNERSHIP | CORPORATION |
|---|---|---|---|
| 1. Easiest to start | _____ | _____ | _____ |
| 2. Limited financial liability | _____ | _____ | _____ |
| 3. Most government regulations and reporting requirements | _____ | _____ | _____ |
| 4. Easiest to dissolve | _____ | _____ | _____ |
| 5. Least opportunity for specialization | _____ | _____ | _____ |
| 6. Separate legal entity | _____ | _____ | _____ |
| 7. Most complicated to form | _____ | _____ | _____ |
| 8. Joint financial liability | _____ | _____ | _____ |
| 9. Special and double taxation | _____ | _____ | _____ |
| 10. Unlimited financial liability | _____ | _____ | _____ |
| 11. Lack of secrecy in operations | _____ | _____ | _____ |
| 12. Frozen investment | _____ | _____ | _____ |
| 13. Easy transer of ownership | _____ | _____ | _____ |
| 14. Long life | _____ | _____ | _____ |

EXERCISE 3-2

(To involve yourself in contemporary business)

Interview a sole proprietor and the partners in a partnership and record their answers to the following questions:

1. Why was this form of business ownership selected?

2. In your opinion, can you attribute any of your present problems to the form of ownership?

3. From your perspective, contrast owner-managers and professional managers.

EXERCISE 3-3

(To help you better understand the use of the library in providing information about businesses)


Table 3-4 in your text lists the 10 largest industrial corporations in the United States.  These firms are compared in terms of sales, assets, net income, number of employees, and net income as a percent of sales.

Go to the library and find the 1981 edition of Moody's Industrial Manual.  In this book, you are to locate the major goods/services produced by the top two largest industrial corporations.

After obtaining this information perpare a brief report detailing the goods/services produced by each firm.

EXERCISE 3-4

(Word Puzzle)

Arranged in a column below is one of the key concepts from this chapter.
Opposite each letter of this key concept is the definition of another
key concept also found in this chapter.  Fill in the blanks provided
with the remaining letter of the defined key concept.

_ _ _ _ _ _ _ _ C _ _ _ _ _          1. It authorizes the forma-
                                        tion of a corporation.

_ _ _ O _ _ _ _ _ _                   2. Voting stock.

_ _ _ _ R _ _ _ _ _ _ _               3. Non-voting stock.

P _ _ _ _                             4. A person appointed to
                                        represent another person.

_ O _ _ _ _ _ _ _ _ _                 5. A special type of tem-
                                        porary partnership.

_ _ _ _ _ _ _ _ R _ _ _              6. The trustee holds the pro-
                                        perty, runs the business,
                                        and accepts funds from
                                        investors.

_ A _ _ _ _ _ _ _ _                   7. An association or two or
                                        more persons to carry on
                                        as co-owners.

_ _ T _ _ _ _ _ _ _ _ _              8. Many savings and loan asso-
                                        ciations are examples.

_ _ _ _ _ _ _ _ _ _ I _ _ _ _ _ _    9. Liability extends to the
                                        owner's personal property.

_ _ _ _ _ _ O _ _ _ _               10. Owners of a corporation.

_ _ _ _ _ _ _ _ N _ _ _ _ _ _ _ _ _  11. Their career is management.

EXERCISE 3-5

(Incident: American Bell)

Answer the questions on a plain piece of paper.

American Telephone and Telegraph (AT&T) Company created a new subsidiary in June 1982 when American Bell was incorporated. American Bell's first product, the Advanced Information System, enables computers made by different manufacturers to exchange data.

American Bell is separate from AT&T. Thus, AT&T's profits from its regulated telephone business cannot be used to help American Bell survive and grow. AT&T is a regulated monopoly. American Bell is in the unregulated, competitive market of computer services.

Questions

1.  IS AT&T an example of public ownership? Explain.

2.  Is AT&T a close corporation or an open corporation? Explain.

3.  In your opinion, is it beneficial for American Bell to be separate from AT&T? Why or why not?

Test Your Business
Vocabulary

1. I (p. 64)      9. J (p. 63)
2. N (p. 68)     10. L (p. 65)
3. P (p. 69)     11. M (p. 88)
4. Q (p. 84)     12. S (p. 74)
5. C (p. 76)     13. E (p. 78)
6. G (p. 76)     14. A (p. 78)
7. R (p. 84)     15. H (p. 72)
8. O (p. 87)

Programmed Review
(refer to the indicated pages
in the text)

1. (p. 63)       6.
2. (p. 63)          A. (p. 84)
3.                  B. (p. 85)
   A. (p. 64)    7.
   B. (p. 68)       A. (p. 86)
   C. (p. 71)       B. (p. 87)
   D. (p. 74)
4.
   A. (p. 74)
   B. (p. 74)
   C. (p. 74)
5.
   A. (p. 82)
   B. (p. 82)
   C. (p. 82)

Exercise 3-1

Sole proprietorship: 1,4,5,10
General partnership: 8,10,12
Corporation: 2,3,6,7,9,11,13,14

Exercise 3-4

1. corporate charter
2. common stock
3. preferred stock
4. proxy
5. joint venture
6. business trust
7. partnership
8. mutual company
9. unlimited liability
10. stockholders
11. professional managers

Test Yourself (Multiple Choice)

1. C (pp. 64-65)    6. B (p. 78)
2. D (p. 74)        7. C (p. 69)
3. C (p. 78)        8. B (p. 86)
4. A (pp. 81-82)    9. D (p. 87)
5. D (pp. 83-84)   10. C (pp. 62-63)

Test Yourself (True-False)

1. False (p. 62)    6. True (p. 72)
2. False (p. 65)    7. False (p. 76)
3. True (p. 86)     8. True (p. 78)
4. True (p. 68)     9. False (p. 84)
5. False (p. 69)   10. True (p. 88)

# Management Functions and Decision Making

Management is an integral part of any organization. It facilitates efforts of organizations in achieving goals through others. This chapter acquaints you with the essentials of basic management.

All managers are charged with the responsibility of effectively and efficiently utilizing the resources of the organization. Managers must have conceptual, people, and technical skills to carry out their responsibilities.

The core of this chapter deals with the five functions of management--planning, organizing, staffing, directing, and controlling. Planning involves setting the firm's objectives and determining how they can be achieved. Organizing relates people, tasks, and resources to each other in order to achieve the stated goals. Staffing is concerned with providing an adequate human resource base for the organization. Directing involves leading, guiding, motivating, and actuating. Controlling encompasses monitoring operations and evaluating performance.

Throughout the chapter various concepts are introduced and discussed. Some examples of these are management by objectives, systems concept, management by exception, job enrichment, and communication. All of these concepts are in some way related to the various functions of management.

The final section in the chapter examines the decision making process. All managers make numerous decisions of varying degrees of complexity. The better the decision making process is, the better the overall management of the organization.

# TEST YOUR BUSINESS VOCABULARY

Test your business vocabulary by matching each key concept with the appropriate phrase. Check your answers with those at the end of this chapter.

## Key Concepts

_____ 1. management
_____ 2. echelons of management
_____ 3. functions of management
_____ 4. strategic planning
_____ 5. operational planning
_____ 6. management by objectives (MBO)
_____ 7. organizing
_____ 8. systems concept

_____ 9. directing
_____ 10. participative management
_____ 11. motivation
_____ 12. job enrichment
_____ 13. leadership
_____ 14. controlling
_____ 15. decision-making process

## Phrases

A. Managers who practice this grant authority to lower-level managers to make routine decisions
B. The process of achieving goals by bringing together and coordinating all organizational resources
C. Planning, organizing, staffing, directing, and controlling
D. The least important of all of the managerial functions
E. A transfer of information between people
F. This function involves monitoring operations and evaluating performance
G. It is related to a manager's ability to get subordinates to develop their capabilities by inspiring them to achieve
H. The different levels or layers of management in an organization
I. This approach starts with recognizing an opportunity or problem and ends with the evaluation stage
J. The ability of an organization to collect and gather information
K. This type of planning is the major responsibility of top-level managers
L. The manager encourages and allows subordinates to involve themselves directly in the decision making that will affect them
M. This type of planning is the primary responsibility of middle- and lower-level managers
N. The management function of recruiting, selecting, training, and promoting personnel to fill both managerial and operating positions.
O. The management function of relating people, tasks, and resources to each other so that a firm can achieve its objectives
P. The result of the drive to satisfy an internal urge
Q. Managing by results
R. A way of looking at a firm as a complex of interacting parts
S. Also called leading, guiding, motivating, or actuating
T. It gives workers more responsibility, authority, and autonomy in planning and doing their work

PROGRAMMED REVIEW

(To help you in understanding the chapter material and to see if you have mastered the objectives stated at the beginning of the chapter)

1.  *Distinguish between managerial work and nonmanagerial work and relate these types of work to the echelons of management.*

    A.  The higher the level of management, the more time a manager spends performing _____ work.

    B.  Assembly-line workers perform _____ work. (Fill in the blank with managerial or nonmanagerial.)

2.  *List and discuss the managerial skills and relate these skills to the echelons of management.*

    A.  The three basic managerial skills are _____, _____, and _____.

    B.  _____ skills are crucial for long-range planning and are most important at the upper echelons of management.

3.  *Discuss the sources of stress on the job and how managers and workers can deal with stress.*

    A.  Four external sources of stress are _____, _____, _____, and _____.

    B.  _____ sources of stress include low self-confidence, poor health, and low tolerance for frustration.

4.  *List and define the functions of management and tell why they are interdependent.*

    A.  The five managerial functions are _____, _____, _____, _____, _____.

    B.  _____ means preparing a firm to cope with the future.

    C.  According to the _____ _____, a firm is a network of interrelationships among the various departments and their environment.

5.  *Discuss the concept of management by objectives.*

A. Management by objectives (MBO) is also known as _____

_____ _____ .

B. Managers who use the MBO approach make the three following assumptions about their subordinates: (1) _____

_____ _____ ,

(2) _____ ,and

(3) _____ .

6. *Interrelate the systems concept to the practice of management.*

A. The marketing, accounting, and personnel departments are _____ of the firm.

B. When a firm accepts social responsibility, it is viewing itself as a subsystem of the larger _____ system.

7. *Contrast Theory X managers and Theory Y managers.*

A. Theory _____ managers assume that the average person is security oriented and indifferent to the needs of the organization.

B. Theory _____ managers assume that the average person is capable of developing interest in his or her work.

8. *Contrast motivational factors and maintenance factors in the motivation-hygiene theory and the theory's relationship to job enrichment.*

A. Achievement, recognition, and responsibility are examples of _____ factors.

B. Pay, working conditions, and job security are examples of _____ factors.

C. _____ _____ gives workers more responsibility, authority, and autonomy in planning and doing their work.

9. *Contrast the "great person" theory of leadership to "traitist theory" and discuss several different types of leadership styles.*

A. The _____ _____ theory of leadership assumes that certain people are gifted with leadership talent and that they would arise as outstanding leaders in any organization.

45

B. The _____ theory of leadership assumes leadership ability can be acquired through experience and learning.

C. Three common types of leadership styles are _____,

_____, and _____.

10. *Illustrate the control process by means of a chart.*

A. The first step in the control process is _____

_____.

B. The final step in the control process is _____

_____.

11. *Discuss the decision-making process and identify the basic types of decisions.*

A. The seven steps in the decision making process are _____

_____, _____,

_____, _____,

_____, _____,

and _____.

B. The two basic types of decisions are _____ and _____.

TEST YOURSELF (Multiple Choice)

Test yourself by selecting the best answer. Check your answer with those at the end of this chapter.

1. Which of the following functions of management is most closely associated with preparing the organization to cope with the future?

A. directing
B. planning
C. organizing
D. controlling

2. Sound organizational objectives should:

A. identify expected results
B. not be expressed in a time frame because this imposes limitations

C. not be attainable so as to provide continuous motivation
D. be stated in general terms

3. Which of the following is not an advantage of management by objectives (MBO)?

   A. subordinates know at the beginning of a planning period what is expected of them
   B. subordinates often enjoy participating with superiors in determining a method for measuring their performance
   C. subordinates are given more opportunity to use new approaches to reaching their objectives since MBO does not predetermine the means for reaching objectives
   D. managers have less confidence in future planning and in predicting results

4. Which one of the following statements is false?

   A. A system is a network of interrelationships among the various departments and their environment.
   B. The systems view underscores the need for top management to set clearly defined goals and to communicate them to lower-level managers and workers.
   C. A systems perspective ignores developments in the external environment.
   D. A systems view of the organization can reduce conflict.

5. The management function that focuses on the recruitment, selection, training, and promotion of personnel is called:

   A. planning
   B. staffing
   C. organizing
   D. directing

6. Which of the following assumptions is characteristic of Theory Y managers?

   A. the average person inherently dislikes work
   B. the average person is, by nature, lazy, irresponsible, and self-centered
   C. the average person is security oriented and indifferent to the needs of the organization
   D. the average person is capable of working productively with a minimum of control and threat of punishment

7. Which of the following is(are) considered to be motivational factors?

   A. growth potential
   B. pay

C. working conditions
D. job security

8. The leadership style that emphasizes the delegation of total responsibility for decision making to subordinates is called:

    A. democratic
    B. autocratic
    C. laissez faire
    D. boss-centered

9. The first stage in the decision making process is:

    A. choosing the best alternative
    B. recognizing an opportunity or problem
    C. evaluating the decision
    D. gathering information

10. According to this concept, routine decisions should be pushed as far down in the firm as possible. This concept is called:

    A. management by objectives
    B. management by results
    C. management by exception
    D. management by analysis

TEST YOURSELF (True-False)

Test yourself by answering whether the following statements are true or false. Check your answers with those at the end of this chapter.

____ 1. A manager who is afraid to delegate would probably be a Theory Y leader.

____ 2. It is generally agreed that there is one best style of leadership.

____ 3. Strategic planning is concerned with a firm's overall strategy of growth and stresses innovation.

____ 4. The systems concept suggests that management should view an organization as a set of separate departments.

____ 5. Job enrichment is the process of redesigning jobs to satisfy higher-level needs and organizational needs by improving worker satisfaction and task efficiency.

____ 6. Management by exception is the same as managing by results.

____ 7. Communication is a transfer of information between people that results in a common understanding between them.

___ 8.  The laissez-faire leadership style is very similar to the auto-
        cratic style.

___ 9.  Technical skills are more important to upper-level managers
        than to lower-level managers.

___ 10. The management function of setting standards of performance,
        measuring actual performance and comparing it to performance
        standards, and taking corrective action is called controlling.

EXERCISE 4-1

(To strengthen your understanding of management by objectives (MBO) )

1.  In your own words, define MBO.



2.  List four advantages of MBO.

    a.

    b.

    c.

    d.

3.  What assumptions about their subordinates do managers make when they use MBO?



4.  List four potential problems in implementing MBO.

    a.

    b.

    c.

    d.

EXERCISE 4-2

(To strengthen your understanding of the applications of motivational factors to management)

1.  Indicate with an X, whether the factors listed on the left are more closely related to hygiene or motivational factors.

| | Hygiene (Maintenance) Factors | Motivational Factors |
|---|---|---|
| A.  Achievement | | |
| B.  Job content factors | | |
| C.  Job context factors | | |
| D.  Recognition | | |
| E.  Working conditions | | |
| F.  Responsibility | | |
| G.  Job security | | |
| H.  Salary | | |
| I.  Advancement | | |
| J.  Nature of supervision | | |

2.  In your own words, discuss the difference between job enrichment and job enlargement.

3.  Can managers use their knowledge of motivation to better design
    jobs in the organization?  Explain.

4.  Why is job rotation important?

EXERCISE 4-3

(To strengthen your understanding of various important management concepts)

Answer on a plain piece of paper.

1. Contrast and give examples of the following types of decisions:

   a. routine decision

   b. nonroutine decision

   c. strategic nonroutine decision

   d. tactical nonroutine decision

2. Describe the following leadership styles:

   a. autocratic

   b. democratic

   c. laissez-faire

3. Is one leadership style better than another one?

4. Using Figure 4-2 in your text as a guide, discuss the relative importance of managerial work at various levels of the management hierarchy.

5. Describe the three managerial skills that are essential for all managers.

EXERCISE 4-4

(Word Puzzle)

Arranged in a column below is one of the key concepts from this chapter. Opposite each letter of this key concept is the definition of another key concept also found in this chapter. Fill in the blanks provided with the remaining letters of the defined key concept.

S _ _ _ _ _ _     1. A concept used in looking at a company as a complex of interrelated parts

_ _ _ T _ _ _ _ _ _ _     2. Measuring performance, comparing with standards, and taking corrective action if required

_ _ R _ _ _ _ _ _     3. Encouraging subordinates to work toward achieving organizational objectives

_ _ A _ _ _ _ _     4. Results in a plan to be followed to reach the desired goals

_ T _ _ _ _ _ _     5. Recruiting, selecting, training, and promoting personnel

_ E _ _ _ _ _ _ _     6. The ability of a person to inspire others to follow him or her

_ _ G _ _ _ _ _ _     7. Relating people, tasks, activities, and resources to accomplish objectives

_ _ _ I _ _ _ _ _     8. Result of a drive to satisfy an internal urge

_ _ _ _ _ _ C _ _ _ _ _     9. A transfer of information that results in understanding

_ _ _ _ _ _ P _ _ _ _     10. Type of management that involves subordinates in decision making

_ _ _ _ _ _ _ _ _ L     11. Planning for the day-to-day survival of an organization

_ _ _ A _ _ _          12. A person who works through
                           others to accomplish objec-
                           tives

_ _ N _ _ _ _ _        13. Planning, organizing, staff-
                           ing, controlling

_ _ N _ _ _ _ _ _      14. As a type, strategic and
                           tactical decisions

_ _ I _ _ _            15. All managers need all three:
                           conceptual, human relations,
                           and technical

_ _ N _ _ _ _ _ _      16. Process of achieving goals
                           by bringing together and
                           coordinating resources of an
                           organization

_ _ _ _ _ G _ _        17. Planning for the long-range
                           future

EXERCISE 4-5

(Incident: A new chairman for General Electric)

Answer the questions on a plain piece of paper.


      Mr. Reginald Jones retired as chairman of General Electric Company in 1981 after a long and distinguished career.  He was succeeded by Mr. John F. Welch, Jr.

      Under Mr. Jones, the company primarily sought respectable profit increases from year to year through the application of GE's time-honored management principles.  Under Mr. Welch, greater emphasis is being placed on competitiveness with foreign competitors and building market share as the keys to long-run profitability.

      Mr. Welch wants GE's product lines, within three to eight years, to be number one or number two in market share in all 250 GE businesses. To accomplish this, he wants GE's managers to be entrepreneurs, not just bureaucrats.  He also wants GE's 400,000 employees (including 25,000 who have "manager" in their titles) to think of the company "as a band of small businesses. . . to take the strength of a large company and act with the agility of a small company."


Questions


1.  Discuss the relative importance of the three managerial skills to Mr. Welch.

2.  Relate the concept of the echelons of management to Mr. Welch's efforts to achieve GE's goals.

3.  Is Mr. Welch more likely to concentrate on operational planning or strategic planning?  Explain.

4.  Do you think Mr. Welch views GE from the systems perspective?  Why or why not?

# CHAPTER 4 ANSWERS

## Test Your Busines Vocabulary

1. B (p. 98)
2. H (p. 99)
3. C (p. 104)
4. K (p. 105)
5. M (p. 105)
6. Q (pp. 105-106)
7. O (p. 107)
8. R (pp. 107-108)
9. S (pp. 108-109
10. L (p. 109)
11. P (pp. 110-111)
12. T (p. 112)
13. G (pp. 112-113)
14. F (p. 115)
15. I (pp. 116-117)

## Programmed Review
(refer to the indicated pages in the text)

1.
  A. (p. 100)
  B. (p. 98)
2.
  A. (p. 101)
  B. (p. 101)
3.
  A. (p. 103)
  B. (p. 103)
4.
  A. (p. 104)
  B. (p. 104)
  C. (p. 107)
5.
  A. (p. 105)
  B. (p. 106)

6.
  A. (p. 108)
  B. (p. 108)
7.
  A. (p. 109)
  B. (p. 109)
8.
  A. (p. 111)
  B. (p. 111)
  C. (p. 112)
9.
  A. (pp. 112-113)
  B. (p. 113)
  C. (p. 113)
10.
  A. (p. 115)
  B. (p. 115)
11.
  A. (pp. 116-117)
  B. (p. 120)

## Exercise 4-2

1. Hygiene factors:
    C, E, G, H, J
2. Motivational factors:
    A, B, D, F, I
3. p. 112
4. pp. 111-112

## Exercise 4-4

1. systems (p. 107)
2. controlling p. 115)
3. directing (p. 108)
4. planning (p. 104)
5. staffing (p. 108)
6. leadership (p.112)
7. organizing (p. 107)
8. motivation (p. 110)
9. communication (p. 110)
10. participative (p. 109)
11. operational (p. 99)
12. manager (p. 98)
13. functions (p. 104)
14. nonroutine (p. 121)
15. skills (p. 101)
16. management (p. 98)
17. strategic (p. 105)

## Test Yourself (Multiple Choice)

1. B (p. 104)
2. A (p. 105)
3. D (p. 106)
4. C (pp. 107-108)
5. B (p. 108)
6. D (p. 109)
7. A (pp. 111-112)
8. C (pp. 113-114)
9. B (p. 117)
10. C (p. 121)

## Test Yourself (True-False)

1. False (p. 109)
2. False (p. 115)
3. True (p. 105)
4. False (pp. 107-108)
5. True (p. 112)
6. False (p. 121)
7. True (p. 110)
8. False (p. 114)
9. False (pp. 101-102)
10. True (p. 115)

# Organizing The Firm

All human endeavors must be organized in order to attain objectives. The business firm is no different from other organizations in this respect. Chapter 5 defines an organization and explains organization as structure. People are an integral part of an organization and their goals must be meshed with those of the firm.

To achieve goals, activities must be grouped and assigned. This is departmentation. The various bases of departmentation are function, geography, product, customer, process, and time. Departmentation is necessary because the number of subordinates a manager can manage is limited. This limitation in the number of persons an individual manager supervises is called span of management.

The next section of the chapter explains the delegation process, which involves entrusting part of a superior's job to a subordinate. The amount of delegation determines how much the power to decide is concentrated. If power is concentrated, the firm is highly centralized. Otherwise, the firm is more decentralized.

Organizations must have structure in order for goals to be achieved. The basic types of organization structures are line, line and staff, and committee. Each one is appropriate for certain situations faced by organizations. Newer approaches to organization, such as the matrix form, allow greater decentralization and less rigid chains of command.

Since individuals are an integral part of the organizing process, their needs must be considered. Maslow has arranged these needs in a hierarchy ranging from physiological needs to self-actualization needs.

The final section of this chapter discusses the informal organization. The informal organization is the entire complex of informal groups that exists within the framework of the formal organization. The informal organization satisfies the social needs of its members.

TEST YOUR BUSINESS VOCABULARY

Test your business vocabulary by matching each key concept with the proper phrase.  Check your answers with those at the end of the chapter.

Key Concepts

___ 1. departmentation
___ 2. span of management
___ 3. delegation
___ 4. decentralization
___ 5. responsibility
___ 6. authority

___ 7. accountability
___ 8. line authority
___ 9. functional authority
___ 10. informal groups
___ 11. organization chart
___ 12. hierarchy of needs
___ 13. staff

Phrases

A.  This concept involves breaking down broad company goals into specific goals for each person in the organization
B.  Identifying, grouping, and assigning activities to specialized departments within an organization
C.  It helps us to understand a firm's structure at a given point in time
D.  Self-actualization is the highest one in this arrangement
E.  The concentration of decision making power at the top level of an organization
F.  Authority of the staff to issue orders directly to line managers
G.  Persons who advise, serve, assist, and support line managers in their work of achieving primary company goals
H.  Something that is structured so that human activity can be coordinated to accomplish objectives
I.  Organizational functions that contribute directly to reaching primary firm goals
J.  The number of subordinates an individual manager supervises
K.  Power to make decisions
L.  The authority relationship that exists between superiors and subordinates
M.  The requirement for subordinates to report results to their superiors
N.  The dispersion of decision making power in an organization
O.  The different levels of management in an organization
P.  The process of entrusting part of a superior's job to a subordinate
Q.  The obligation of a subordinate to perform an assigned task
R.  They arise naturally as a result of human interaction on the job


PROGRAMMED REVIEW

(To help you in understanding the chapter material and to see if you have mastered the objectives stated at the beginning of the chapter)

1. *Tell the difference between personal and organizational objectives and explain how they are integrated.*

   A. Organizations _____ objectives when they settle for less than the total achievement of all the objectives of their publics.

   B. A _____ is necessary since neither the worker's objective nor the firm's objective will be achieved 100 percent.

2. *Draw a figure that illustrates the hierarchy of organizational objectives.*

   A. The number of levels of objectives depends on the firm's _____ and complexity.

   B. The concept of hierarchy of objectives involves breaking down _____ company goals into _____ goals for each person in the organization.

3. *List and give an example of the different bases for departmentation.*

   A. The six major bases of departmentation are _____, _____, _____, _____, _____, and _____.

   B. General Motors has separate divisions for Pontiac, Oldsmobile, Chevrolet, Buick, and Cadillac. This is an example of _____ departmentation.

4. *List and explain the factors that affect a manager's optimum span of management.*

   A. Theory _____ managers tend to have narrower spans of management than Theory _____ managers.

   B. The subordinates' training and _____ to work with others can influence the span of management.

5. *List and explain the three actions involved in the delegation process.*

   A. The three actions involved in the delegation process are _____ _____, _____ _____, and _____ _____.

B. _____ is the right to take the action necessary to accomplish an assigned task.

6. *Relate the delegation process to the degree to which a firm is centralized or decentralized.*

   A. _____ of authority means that decision-making authority is concentrated in the hands of a few people at the top level of a firm.

   B. _____ of authority means that decision-making authority is spread throughout the firm.

7. *Compare the line, line and staff, and committee organization structures and discuss the matrix organization and quality-of-work-life programs.*

   A. _____ functions contribute directly to reaching primary firm goals.

   B. _____ are people who advise and assist line managers to achieve company objectives.

   C. In the _____ organizational structure, several people share authority and responsibility for accomplishing an objective.

   D. A _____ organization includes horizontal reporting requirements in addition to the traditional vertical chain of command.

8. *Tell the difference between line function and staff function and line managers and staff people.*

   A. In a typical manufacturing firm, production and marketing are considered _____ functions.

   B. The _____ staff performs duties at the request of his or her line boss.

9. *Draw an organization chart and tell what it indicates and does not indicate.*

   A. An organization chart graphically depicts a firm's _____ structure at a given point in time.

   B. The lines of _____ or chain of command can be found on the organization chart.

10. *Discuss the hierarchy of human needs.*

   A. The hierarchy is based on the _____ of needs.

   B. The five levels of needs in the hierarchy are _____,

   _____, _____, _____, and _____.

11. *Compare formal and informal organizations.*

   A. Human interaction in the _____ organization is structured by management.

   B. The employee grapevine is a characteristic of the _____ organization.


TEST YOURSELF (Multiple Choice)

Test yourself by selecting the best answer.  Check your answers with those at the end of this chapter.

1. Because an organization's objectives sometimes conflict with the personal objectives of its employees, the firm must:

   A. ignore employee objectives
   B. suboptimize objectives
   C. ignore organizational objectives
   D. not permit managers to delegate authority

2. The three basic components that must be related to each other through the process of organizing are:

   A. time, people, and money
   B. physical resources, time, and people
   C. people, activities, and physical resources
   D. activities, people, and time

3. Which of the following least affects a manager's span of management?

   A. the motivation of his or her subordinates
   B. the pace of technology
   C. the capacity of the manager
   D. the income of subordinates

4. The highest level of need in the hierarchy of human needs is:

   A. the need to belong
   B. the need for self-actualization

C. the need for esteem
D. the need for safety

5. Which of the following is a major advantage of the line organization?

   A. the ease of understanding the organizational structure
   B. the amount of paperwork required
   C. the need for the supervisor to be an expert in many areas
   D. the attitudes of subordinates toward this type of organization

6. The organization chart indicates all of the following except:

   A. the lines of authority
   B. how the firm is departmented
   C. the various positions in the firm
   D. the nature of the informal relationships in the organization

7. The central concern of the informal dimension of the business organization is:

   A. profit
   B. economic needs
   C. human interaction
   D. chain of command

8. Which one of these is not a basis upon which an organization can be departmented?

   A. style
   B. function
   C. time
   D. process

9. Staff people:

   A. delegate to line people
   B. advise and serve line people
   C. are inferior in status to line people
   D. make up the chain of command

10. Which of the following are likely to be line functions in a manufacturing company?

   A. production and marketing
   B. lending and collecting
   C. quality control and market research
   D. advertising

TEST YOURSELF (True-False)

Test yourself by answering whether the following statements are true or false. Check your answers with those at the end of this chapter.

___ 1. Suboptimization means that business firms must settle for less than the total achievement of all the objectives of their publics.

___ 2. Activities are the connecting link between an organization's objectives and its structure.

___ 3. Accountability is the obligation of a subordinate to whom a job has been assigned to do it.

___ 4. The hierarchy of organizational objectives involves breaking down broad company goals into specific goals for each person in the organization.

___ 5. It is generally believed that smaller spans of management are more practical at lower levels in the firm.

___ 6. Responsibility and authority are conceptually the same.

___ 7. Theory Y managers are more likely to delegate authority than are Theory X managers.

___ 8. Line persons serve as advisors and assistants to staff individuals.

___ 9. Members seek to satisfy social needs in the informal organization.

___ 10. The physiological needs are the most prepotent of all human needs.

EXERCISE 5-1

(To help you understand the concept of departmentation)

1. Label the following examples according to the nature of the departmentation.  Each example should be labeled function, geography, product, customer, process, or time.

   Example                                    Basis of Departmentation

   A.  Miller Brewing Co. with both
       cooking and aging departments.         _____

   B.  A local community college
       with regular day classes and
       a strong evening division.             _____

   C.  Exxon Corporation with explora-
       tion, production, refining,
       marketing, and finance depart-
       ments.                                 _____

   D.  General Motors with separate
       divisions for Buick, Cadillac,
       Chevrolet, Oldsmobile, and
       Pontiac.                               _____

   E.  Boeing Corporation with separate
       divisions for the commercial
       aviation and defense markets.          _____

   F.  Internal Revenue Service with
       offices in various regions of
       the country.                           _____

EXERCISE 5-2

(To strengthen your understanding of three basic types of organizational structures)

Place an X in the space under the type of organizational structure(s) to which the phrase applies:

| | Line Organization | Line and Staff Organization | Committee Organization |
|---|---|---|---|
| 1. Often exists within the other two types | _____ | _____ | _____ |
| 2. Oldest and simplest | _____ | _____ | _____ |
| 3. Greatest potential for buck-passing | _____ | _____ | _____ |
| 4. Program management | _____ | _____ | _____ |
| 5. Least potential for buck-passing | _____ | _____ | _____ |
| 6. Personal biases in decision making are reduced | _____ | _____ | _____ |
| 7. Maximum potential for the creation of unnecessary staff positions | _____ | _____ | _____ |
| 8. Group management | _____ | _____ | _____ |
| 9. Frees line manager to devote more energy to line functions | _____ | _____ | _____ |
| 10. No specialists to whom to turn for advice | _____ | _____ | _____ |
| 11. No functional authority | _____ | _____ | _____ |
| 12. Team management | _____ | _____ | _____ |

EXERCISE 5-3

(To better understand line and staff relationships)

1. Conflict between line and staff is a major problem area. Another area of conflict is between line functions. To help you understand the nature of this problem, read "Can Marketing and Manufacturing Coexist?", Harvard Business Review (September-October 1977). After reading the article, explain (in the space provided) the basic causes of the problem.

2. "Business firms are becoming increasingly less productive because of the proliferation of staff personnel." Do you agree or disagree with the above statement? Why or why not?

EXERCISE 5-4

(Word Puzzle)

Arranged in a column below is one of the key concepts from this chapter. Opposite each letter of this key concept is the definition of another important term used in the chapter, although not necessarily a key concept. Fill in the blanks provided with the remaining letters of the appropriate term.

_ _ L _ _ _ _ _ _ _

1. The process of entrusting part of a superior's job to a subordinate.

_ _ _ _ _ I _ _ _ _ _ _

2. Something that is structured so that human activity can be coordinated to accomplish objectives.

_ _ N _ _ _ _ _ _ _ _ _

3. The concentration of decision-making power at the top level of an organization.

_ E _ _ _ _ _ _ _ _ _ _

4. The obligation of a subordinate to perform an assigned task.

A _ _ _ _ _ _ _

5. The right to take the action necessary to accomplish an assigned task.

_ _ _ N _ _ _ _ _ _ _ _ _

6. The number of subordinates a manager manages.

D _ _ _ _ _ _ _ _ _ _ _ _ _

7. The dispersion of decision making power in an organization.

_ _ _ _ _ S _

8. One of the bases for departmentation, such as might be used by a brewery.

T _ _ _

9. One of the bases for departmentation, such as might be used by a college that operates day classes and an evening division.

_ A _ _ _ _

10. Evolving type of organizational structure that includes horizontal reporting requirements.

_ _ F _ _ _ _ _

11. These groups exist outside the formal organizational structure.

_ _ _ F _

12. Two types are personalized and specialized.

EXERCISE 5-5

(Incident: The Space Command)

Answer the questions on a plain piece of paper.


In line with its plans to increase the military use of outer space, the U.S. Air Force has recently created a separate command, the Space Command, to carry out space missions. The reason for the creation of the Space Command is to ensure that a single commander would be responsible for Air Force space operations.

Prior to the creation of the new command, responsibility for such space missions as spy satellite launches was assigned to the Air Force's research groups. The new command also puts space missions on an equal footing with tactical and strategic air operations within the Air Force hierarchy.

Questions

1.  Is the concept of the hierarchy of organizational objectives relevant to nonbusiness organizations such as the Air Force? Why or why not?

2.  Is the process of departmentation relevant to nonbusiness organizations such as the Air Force? Why or why not?

3.  Would you describe the U.S. Air Force as a line and staff organization or a committee organization? Explain.

4.  Are military organizations likely to be more centralized organizations than business organizations? Why or why not?

# CHAPTER 5 ANSWERS

## Test Your Business Vocabulary

1. B (p. 132)
2. J (p. 134)
3. P (p. 137)
4. N (p. 138)
5. Q (p. 137)
6. K (p. 137)
7. M (p. 137)
8. L (p. 139)
9. F (p. 142)
10. R (p. 151)
11. C (p. 139)
12. D (p. 148)
13. G (p. 141)

## Programmed Review
(refer to the indicated pages in the text)

1.
  A (p. 130)
  B (p. 130)
2.
  A (p. 132)
  B (p. 132)
3.
  A (p. 133)
  B (p. 133)
4.
  A (p. 135)
  B (p. 135)
5.
  A (p. 137)
  B (p. 137)

6.
  A (p. 138)
  B (p. 138)
7.
  A (p. 141)
  B (p. 142)
  C (p. 144)
  D (p. 145)
8.
  A (p. 141)
  B (p. 141)
9.
  A (p. 138)
  B (p. 139)
10.
  A (p. 148)
  B (p. 149)
11.
  A (p. 152)
  B (p. 152)

## Exercise 5-1

(p. 133)

A. process
B. time
C. function
D. product
E. customer
F. geography

## Exercise 5-4

1. delegation (p. 137)
2. organization (p. 129)
3. centralization (p. 138)
4. responsibility (p. 137)
5. authority (p. 137)
6. span of management (p. 134)
7. decentralization (p. 138)
8. process (p. 133)
9. time (p. 133)
10. matrix (p. 145)
11. informal (p. 151)
12. staff (p. 141)

## Test Yourself (Multiple Choice)

1. B (p. 130)
2. C (p. 131)
3. D (p. 135)
4. B (p. 148)
5. A (p. 139)
6. D (p. 138)
7. C (pp. 151-154)
8. A (p. 133)
9. B (p. 141)
10. A (p. 141)

## Test Yourself (True-False)

1. True (p. 130)
2. True (p. 131)
3. False (p. 137)
4. True (p. 132)
5. False (p. 135)
6. False (p. 137)
7. True (p. 135)
8. False P. 141)
9. True (pp. 151-152)
10. True (p. 148)

# CHAPTER 6

# Personnel
# Management

Chapter 6 addresses the major concepts related to the most important resource in the organization - the human resource. Many people believe the human resource is the most flexible and the most productive of all the resources. If this is true, the organization should carefully manage efforts in recruiting, selecting, training, developing, appraising, and compensating. In most organizations, the personnel department manages these activities.

The chapter initiates the discussion with the determination of human resource needs. This is done in conjunction with a thorough understanding of company objectives. After conducting job analyses and developing job descriptions and job specifications, the next step in this process involves searching for and recruiting applicants. The various methods and approaches to recruiting and selecting may vary depending on the nature of the organization. Following selection, training and development takes place. Training and development are continuous processes that are necessary for the organization to achieve its objectives.

The final sections of the chapter examine appraising employee performance, compensation, promotion, personnel services, and termination. An effective performance appraisal system allows the firm to assess the contribution of employees. In addition to appraisal, employees must be compensated. In many cases, compensation is based on the employee's contribution or importance to the firm. Those employees that perform well are considered for promotion to higher positions, usually with more pay and more challenge. Employees may be terminated because of dismissal, death, retirement, or voluntary resignation.

In summary, this chapter covers a number of interrelated activities that must be performed to acquire, motivate, and retain qualified personnel in the organization. The management of the personnel task is probably one of the most challenging in the firm.

# TEST YOUR BUSINESS VOCABULARY

Test your business vocabulary by matching each key concept with the proper phrase. Check your answers with those at the end of the chapter.

## Key Concepts

___ 1. job analysis
___ 2. job description
___ 3. job specification
___ 4. in-depth interview
___ 5. job-skill training
___ 6. organization development (OD)
___ 7. performance appraisal system
___ 8. piece rate
___ 9. wage
___ 10. salary
___ 11. exit interview
___ 12. promotion
___ 13. affirmative action plan
___ 14. human resource
___ 15. personnel management

## Phrases

A. a re-education process that is used to change the culture, values, and behavior of the entire organization in order to improve its effectiveness

B. Efforts to prepare people for managerial positions and to improve the managerial skills of present managers

C. Its purpose is to find out the reasons an employee leaves the firm

D. The personnel who staff a firm, including both workers and managers

E. An approach to job fairs

F. A statement of the personal qualifications needed by the person who is to fill each job

G. Its main purpose is to teach specific job skills

H. The task of attracting potential employees to a firm

I. Fixed compensation to an employee who is regularly paid on a weekly, biweekly, or monthly basis

J. A method of paying workers based on units of output

K. Top management's efforts to develop good company personnel, including both managers and workers

L. The task of implementing top management's policies regarding human resource management

M. A listing of the nature and requirements of a job

N. The purpose is to encourage and reward increased employee productivity

O. A detailed statement by a firm describing how the firm will implement a program of actively recruiting members of minority groups and women and upgrading jobs currently held by them

P. Defining the jobs that must be done if a firm is to reach its goals

Q. Moving up to a higher position in the firm

R. Compensation to a worker who is paid by the hour

S. A system used by management to measure and evaluate employee performance on the job

T. The interview given to an applicant who passes the selection tests

U. A job applicant's first interview with a prospective employer

PROGRAMMED REVIEW

(To help you in understanding the chapter material and to see if you have mastered the objectives stated at the beginning of the chapter)

1. *Explain the meaning of human resource management.*

   A. A firm's most important resource or _____ is its human resource.

   B. Managing the human resource requires great skill because people are different in terms of their _____, _____, and _____.

2. *Identify and discuss the major tasks of personnel management.*

   A. Personnel management consists of _____ _____ _____ _____

   B. A _____ _____ is a staff department that is created to advise and help line managers to manage their personnel.

3. *Discuss government and private efforts to eliminate discrimination in employment.*

   A. An _____ _____ _____ is a firm's detailed statement describing how it will go about actively recruiting members of minority groups and women and upgrading jobs currently held by them.

   B. The _____ Act, as amended in 1978, prohibits employers to engage in job discrimination against people between ages 40 and 70.

4. *Differentiate among the three types of interviews used in the selection process and discuss selection tests.*

   A. The three types of interviews used in the selection process are _____, _____, and _____.

B. The five basic types of selection tests are _____

_____

_____ .

5. *Compare job-skill training, management development, and organization development.*

A. _____ _____ refers to efforts to prepare people for managerial positions and to improve the managerial skills of present managers.

B. _____-_____ training teaches employees specific job skills.

C. Organization development is a _____ process that is used to change the _____ and _____ of the entire organization.

6. *Compare the merit rating system with the management by objectives approach to appraising employee performance.*

A. In the merit rating system, each employee's _____ _____ is appraised every six months or every year.

B. The _____ _____ _____ approach to rating employee performance requires mutual trust and respect.

7. *Discuss wage and salary administration and pay equity.*

A. _____ and _____ _____ is the process of developing and implementing a sound and fair method of compensating employees.

B. To encourage greater worker productivity, some firms offer _____ pay.

C. A worker paid a fixed amount on a weekly, biweekly, or monthly basis receives a _____.

D. _____ is the perceived fairness of what a worker does compared to what he or she receives from the employer.

8. *Discuss the issues involved in determining an employee's promotability.*

A.   A _____ means moving up to a higher position in the firm.

B.   _____ in the present job should be the basic factor in determining an employee's promotability to a higher job.

9. *Give examples of the personnel services that personnel departments provide to the firm and its employees.*

A.   Examples of personnel services include _____

_____

_____

B.   The _____ manual is generally prepared by the personnel department along with upper-level managers.

10. *Identify the issues involved in terminating employees.*

A.   _____ is an involuntary, temporary or permanent separation of the employee.

B.   _____ is a permanent involuntary separation due to a permanent layoff or outright firing of an employee.


TEST YOURSELF (Multiple Choice)

Test yourself by selecting the best answer.  Check your answers with those at the end of this chapter.

1. Which of the following is <u>not</u> one of the major tasks of personnel management?

   A.   determining human resource needs
   B.   compensating employees
   C.   measuring market shares
   D.   appraising employee performance

2. This document states the personal qualifications needed by the person who is to fill each job.  It is called a:

   A.   job order
   B.   job specification
   C.   job analysis
   D.   job description

76

3. Which of the following antidiscrimination laws prohibits job discrimination based on race, color, religion, sex, or national origin?

   A. Equal Pay Act (1963)
   B. Executive Order 11246 (1965)
   C. Age Discrimination in Employment Act (1967)
   D. Civil Rights Act (1965)

4. A test that measures general verbal ability is a form of:

   A. intelligence test
   B. aptitude test
   C. performance test
   D. personality test

5. The bona fide occupational qualificiation (BFOQ) is most important in preparing:

   A. job specifications
   B. job descriptions
   C. personality tests
   D. aptitude tests

6. Performance appraisal training:

   A. helps a worker to rate his or her job performance
   B. helps a worker to rate his or her superior's job performance
   C. helps a manager to be less sensitive to subordinates
   D. helps a manager to rate subordinates' job performance more objectively

7. An involuntary temporary or permanent separation of an employee due to a temporary business slack would probably be an example of:

   A. dismissal
   B. discharge
   C. resignation
   D. retirement

8. The type of compensation where the worker is paid a certain rate for each acceptable unit of output is called:

   A. a wage
   B. a salary
   C. a piece rate
   D. incentive pay

9. Which one of the following is not a main feature of wage and salary administration?

A. wage and salary surveys
B. job evaluation
C. affirmative action recruiting
D. performance rating

10. The theory that considers the perceived fairness of what a worker does compared to what he or she receives from the employer is called:

A. expectancy theory
B. equity theory
C. content theory
D. exchange theory

TEST YOURSELF (True-False)

Test yourself by answering whether the following statements are true or false. Check your answers with those at the end of this chapter.

____ 1. Job-skill training teaches employees specific job skills.

____ 2. Management development is a re-education process that is used to change the cultures, values, and behavior of the entire organization in order to improve its effectiveness.

____ 3. Job evaluation is a method for determining the relationship between pay rates for particular job classifications.

____ 4. A worker paid on an hourly rated basis receives a wage.

____ 5. Performance tests measure ability such as mechanical or clerical aptitude.

____ 6. Due to excessive costs, recruiting should not be a continuous process for most medium- and large-sized firms.

____ 7. A discharge is a permanent involuntary separation due to a permanent layoff or firing of an employee.

____ 8. A poor indicator of human resource planning is stability of employment.

____ 9. Selection tests are used to measure an applicant's potential to perform the job for which he or she is being considered.

____ 10. T-group training is one of the newer techniques used in management development programs.

EXERCISE 6-1

(To help you understand the legal aspects of personnel management)

1.  Discuss the general purposes of the antidiscrimination legislation.

2.  Briefly describe, in your own words, the intent of the following specific pieces of legislation:

    A.  Equal Pay Act (1963)

    B.  Civil Rights Act (1964)

    C.  Executive Order 11246 (1965)

    D.  Age Discrimination in Employment Act (1967)

    E.  Rehabilitation Act (1973)

3.  Discuss the underlying philosophy of affirmative action recruiting programs.

EXERCISE 6-2

(To involve yourself in contemporary business)

1. Visit your school library.  Write a one-page report on the differences between "positions available" ads in your hometown newspaper and *The Wall Street Journal*.

2. Assume that you want your instructor to write a reference letter on your behalf and send it to a prospective employer.  Write the letter for the instructor in the space below.

EXERCISE 6-3

(To enhance your understanding of personnel management tasks)

Briefly describe the major concerns under each of the following personnel management tasks:

1. Determining human resource needs

2. Searching for and recruiting applicants to fill those needs

3. Selecting applicants for employment

4. Training and developing personnel

5. Appraising employee performance

6. Compensating employees

7. Promoting employees

8. Providing personnel services

9. Terminating employees

EXERCISE 6-4

(Crossword Puzzle Review)

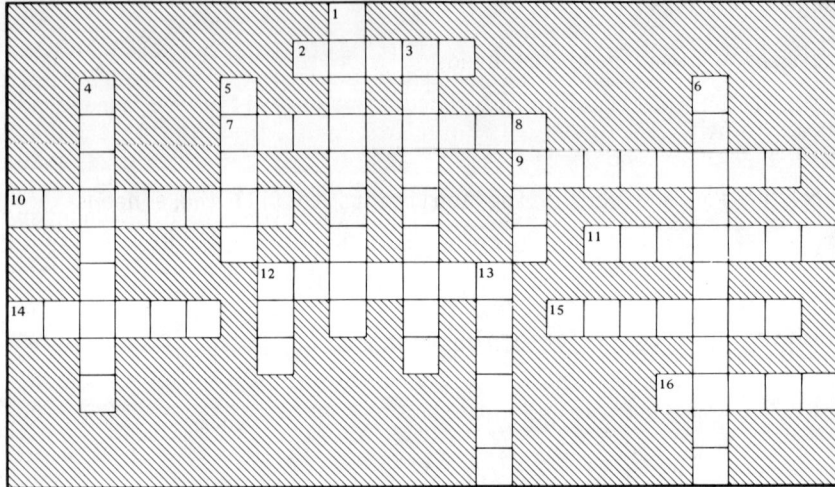

## Across

2. A rating system used to evaluate employee performance
7. One type is the job applicant's final selection _____
9. Defining jobs that must be done if a firm is to reach its goals; used with the word "job"
10. The personnel who staff a firm; in asset terms, they are the human _____
11. To attract potential employees to a firm
12. To move someone up to a higher position on a firm's job ladder
14. One who has been on the job longer than someone else is this to them
15. Type of interview given to someone who passes selection tests
16. Last in a series of interviews of a prospective employee

## Down

1. Tests which include aptitude, intelligence, and performance
3. The goods store owners have in stock at a certain point in time
4. Human resource function; manager, management, department.
5. A method of paying workers in which a certain amount is paid for each acceptable unit of output
6. Prepared from the job analysis, lists the requirements of a job
8. Paid to a worker who works on an hourly basis
12. Money a worker receives under an incentive plan; incentive _____
13. To hire an individual; to make use of someone's services

EXERCISE 6-5

(Incident: Headhunting)

Answer the questions on a plain piece of paper.


Many firms use outside recruitment firms (headhunters) in their search for and recruitment of managers. Traditionally, headhunters have limited their searching and recruiting activities to managers who are employed. The underlying philosophy is that the best managers available are those who are working. Unemployed managers were assumed to be unemployed because of their shortcomings as managers.

In the recession of the early 1980s, however, some headhunters began to include unemployed managers in their search and recruitment efforts. These headhunters believed that a growing number of managers were unemployed for reasons beyond their control and that the overall quality of the unemployed managers was increasing. Furthermore, unemployed managers are available for hire almost immediately while those who are employed require more time to make the move to another company. Some headhunters also claim that unemployed managers are more willing to relocate.

Questions

1. Why would a firm hire a headhunter to search for and recruit managers?

2. Is it ethical for firms to use headhunters to recruit managers away from other employers? Why or why not?

3. If you were a headhunter, would you limit your searching and recruiting efforts to managers who are working for other employers or would you also search and recruit among the ranks of the unemployed managers? Explain.

# CHAPTER 6 ANSWERS

## Test Your Business Vocabulary

| | |
|---|---|
| 1. P (p. 168) | 9. R (p. 183) |
| 2. M (p. 169) | 10. I (p. 183) |
| 3. F (p. 169) | 11. C (p. 188) |
| 4. T (p. 175) | 12. Q (p. 185) |
| 5. G (p. 178) | 13. O (p. 171) |
| 6. A (p. 180) | 14. D (p. 164) |
| 7. S (pp. 180-181) | 15. L (p. 164) |
| 8. J (p. 182) | |

## Programmed Review
(refer to the indicated pages in the text)

1.
   A. (p. 164)
   B. (p. 164)
2.
   A. (p. 164)
   B. (p. 165)
3.
   A. (p. 171)
   B. (p. 172)
4.
   A. (pp. 174-176)
   B. (p. 175)
5.
   A. (p. 179)
   B. (p. 178)
   C. (p. 180)

6.
   A. (p. 181)
   B. (p. 182)
7.
   A. (p. 182)
   B. (p. 182)
   C. (p. 183)
   D. (p. 184)
8.
   A. (p. 185)
   B. (p. 185)
9.
   A. (p. 186)
   B. (pp. 185-186)
10.
   A. (p. 188)
   B. (p. 189)

## Exercise 6-1

1. (pp. 172-173)
2. (p. 172)
3. (pp. 171-173)

## Exercise 6-4

Down:

1. selection (p. 175)
3. inventory (p. 175)
4. personnel (p. 164)
5. piece (p. 182)
6. description
8. wage (p. 183)
12. pay (p. 182)
13. employ

Across:

2. merit (p. 181)
7. interview (p. 176)
9. analysis (p. 168)
10. resource (p. 164)
11. recruit (p. 170)
12. promote (p. 185)
14. senior
15. indepth (p. 175)
16. final P. 176)

## Test Yourself (Multiple Choice)

1. C (p. 164)
2. B (p. 169)
3. D (p. 172)
4. A (p. 175)
5. A (p. 176)
6. D (pp. 180-181)
7. A (pp. 188-189)
8. C (p. 182)
9. C (p. 183)
10. B (p. 184)

## Test Yourself (True-False)

1. True (p. 178)
2. False (p. 179)
3. True (P. 183)
4. True (p. 183)
5. False (p. 175)
6. False (pp. 170-171)
7. True (p. 189)
8. False (p. 166)
9. True (p. 174)
10. True (pp. 179-180)

## CHAPTER 7

# Labor Relations

Chapter 7 is designed to acquaint you with concepts and ideas concerning labor law and unions. In most organizations, employees feel the need for protection and security. Thus, the chapter begins with a discussion of the purposes of unionization and a brief history of the movement in the United States.

The next section elaborates on specific pieces of legislation, such as the Wagner Act (which lists employer practices that are unfair to labor) and the Taft-Hartley Act (which lists several practices that are unfair for unions to commit). Each item of legislation provides guidelines for labor or management or both.

Like business firms, unions have organized structures. The two basic types of unions are craft (organized according to trade) and industrial (organized according to industries). In addition, unions may be organized at local, national, and federation levels.

The chapter concludes with a detailed analysis of the various sources of labor-management conflict. Some of the key issues involved in the conflict are jobs, seniority, productivity, and inflation. In all of the conflicts, both labor and management have weapons to use. Some of labor's main weapons are strikes, pickets, and boycotts. Management's main weapons are lockouts, layoffs, and injunctions.

# TEST YOUR BUSINESS VOCABULARY

Test your business vocabulary by matching each key concept with the proper phrase. Check your answers with those at the end of the chapter.

## Key Concepts

_____ 1. collective bargaining
_____ 2. blacklists
_____ 3. injunction
_____ 4. craft unions
_____ 5. industrial unions
_____ 6. closed shop

_____ 7. agency shop
_____ 8. right-to-work laws
_____ 9. mediation
_____ 10. supplemental unemployment benefits (SUB)
_____ 11. compulsory arbitration
_____ 12. boycott

## Phrases

A. Used only when essential public services are involved
B. A neutral third party tries to prevent negotiations from breaking down
C. An order issued by a court
D. State laws permitted under the Taft-Hartley Act that outlaw the union shop type of union security
E. A temporary withdrawal of all or some employees from an employer's service
F. Employees need not join or pay dues to a union
G. Only members of the union can be hired by an employer
H. The process of negotiating a labor contract between union representatives and employer representatives
I. Membership is restricted to workers with specific skills
J. The union tries to get people to refuse to deal with the firm
K. All employees for whom the union bargains must pay dues but need not join
L. Payments to laid-off workers made by their employers
M. A provision in a collective bargaining agreement that maintains the worker's income at some agreed-upon level during a year
N. Lists circulated among employers containing the names of workers who were known to be in favor of unions
O. Lists circulated among workers containing the names of employers whom unions considered unfair to workers because they refused to hire union members
P. Include semiskilled and unskilled workers
Q. A neutral party suggests a possible compromise of the dispute

PROGRAMMED REVIEW

(To help you in understanding the chapter material and to see if you
have mastered the objectives stated at the beginning of the chapter)

1. *Outline the history of unionism in the United States.*

   A. The economic philosophy of _____-_____ was at the
      heart of our eocnomic system until the 1930s.

   B. The _____ _____ of the 1800s brought numerous changes
      to the working world, such as big factories and mechanization,
      which in turn intensified unionization efforts.

2. *List the major federal labor laws and discuss the major provisions
   of each.*

   A. The _____-_____ Act prohibits employers from using an
      injunction unless they can meet the requirements set out in the
      act.

   B. The _____-_____ Act is a "promanagement" act that
      lists several practices that are unfair for unions to commit.

   C. The _____ Act is often called labor's "Magna Charta."

3. *Identify the general reasons workers join unions and explain how
   unions are organized.*

   A. Union members are represented in collective _____ by pro-
      fessional negotiators.

   B. The two basic types of union are _____ and _____
      unions.

   C. The _____ union in the basic unit of union organization.

4. *Discuss the National Labor Relations Board's role in certifying a
   union.*

   A. The National Labor Relations Board (NLRB) conducts _____
      to determine if workers wish to be represented by a union.

   B. If an industrial union is seeking to organize workers at a
      local plant, signed authorization cards must be secured from at
      least _____ percent of the employees.

5. *Give examples of union objectives.*

   A. The _____ annual wage is a provision in a labor contract
      that maintains the workers' income level during a year.

87

B. The strongest type of union security is the _____ shop.

C. _____ is efforts by a group of people who have the same special interest.

6. *Cite specific issues that might lead to labor-management conflict.*

   A. The six basic sources of labor-management conflict are _____

   _____

   _____

   _____

   _____

   B. An _____ _____ means that wage hikes will be granted on the basis of changes in the cost of living.

7. *Explain how employees and employers bargain collectively through union and management representatives.*

   A. In _____, the neutral third party's task is to prevent negotiations from breaking down.

   B. In _____, the neutral third party's task is to suggest a possible compromise.

   C. In voluntary _____, a neutral third party hears both sides of the dispute and settles the issue.

8. *List and discuss labor and management's "weapons" in dealing with conflict.*

   A. Labor's main weapons are _____

   _____.

   B. Management's main weapons are the _____

   _____.

9. *Appraise the future prospects for the union movement in the United States.*

   A. _____-collar workers now account for more than half of our labor force, representing a prime opportunity for unionization.

   B. The future of unions in the United States will depend largely on the success with which they can organize people in

_____ areas, _____, and occupations that traditionally have not been unionized.

TEST YOURSELF (Multiple Choice)

Test yourself by selecting the best answer.  Check your answers with
those at the end of this chapter.

1.  The basic unit of union organization is the:

    A.  national union
    B.  regional union
    C.  union federation
    D.  local union

2.  In a _____ shop, all employees for whom the union bargains must
    pay dues but need not join.

    A.  open shop
    B.  agency shop
    C.  closed shop
    D.  security shop

3.  In labor negotiations, when a neutral third party hears both sides
    of the dispute and settles the issue with both parties agreeing to
    abide by his or her decision, this is called:

    A.  conciliation
    B.  mediation
    C.  arbitration
    D.  compensation

4.  Which of the following acts allows the National Labor Relations
    Board (NLRB) to secure a federal court injunction against unions
    that engage in illegal strike, picket, and/or boycott activity?

    A.  Taft-Hartley Act
    B.  Norris-LaGuardia Act
    C.  Landrum-Griffin Act
    D.  Closed Shop Act

5.  Payments made by employers to workers who have been laid off are
    called:

    A.  strike benefits
    B.  state unemployment compensation
    C.  supplemental unemployment benefits
    D.  seniority compensation

6. Paying workers for work they do not perform is often called:

   A. featherbedding
   B. blacklisting
   C. closed shop payments
   D. discriminatory payment practices

7. In trying to protect their members against reduced buying power due to inflation, many unions have sought:

   A. grievance procedures
   B. seniority provisions
   C. escalator clauses
   D. right-to-work laws

8. Which of the following is _not_ a weapon that can be used by management to counter labor's threat to organize or strike?

   A. the lockout
   B. the layoff
   C. the injunction
   D. the protection of the Fair Labor Standards Act (1938)

9. When unions attempt to get people to refuse to deal with the boycotted firm's customers and suppliers, this is known as:

   A. a primary boycott
   B. a secondary boycott
   C. an original boycott
   D. a tertiary boycott

10. A strike is:

   A. a permanent withdrawal of employees
   B. the most frequently used method of settling labor disputes
   C. the same as a boycott
   D. the union's ultimate weapon

TEST YOURSELF (True-False)

Test yourself by answering whether the following statements are true or false. Check your answers with those at the end of this chapter.

____ 1. In a closed shop an employer can hire only union members.

____ 2. The Taft-Hartley Act is a "pro-union" act that lists several practices that are unfair for management to commit.

____ 3. Mediation means the same as arbitration.

____ 4. The legality of secondary boycotts depends on their purpose and the means used to carry them out.

____ 5. The majority of labor and management disputes end in strikes.

____ 6. Right-to-work laws outlaw the union shop.

____ 7. The contract negotiated between employer and union representatives is called the collective bargaining agreement.

____ 8. Compulsory arbitration is used only when essential public services are involved.

____ 9. Within the context of labor relations, all complaints are considered as grievances.

____ 10. Unfair lists contained the names of workers who were known to be in favor of unions.

EXERCISE 7-1

(To review the provisions of major labor laws)

Match each legal provision with the proper law.

A.  Norris-LaGuardia Act
B.  Wagner Act
C.  Fair Labor Standards Act
D.  Taft-Hartley Act
E.  Landrum-Griffin Act

____ 1. Outlaws the closed shop

____ 2. Outlaws the yellow-dog contract

____ 3. Established the National Labor Relations Board

____ 4. Established a federal minimum wage

____ 5. Severely limits the employer's use of the labor injunction

____ 6. Permits the states to pass right-to-work laws

____ 7. Requires unions to bargain in good faith with employers

____ 8. Lists employer practices, that are unfair to labor

____ 9. Defines the normal work week

____ 10. Designed to ensure democratic operation of unions

____ 11. Makes it illegal for unions to coerce workers to join

____ 12. Provides for injunctive processes in illegal strikes

____ 13. Sets up rules for electing union officers

____ 14. Prohibits unions from setting excessive dues

EXERCISE 7-2

(To strengthen your understanding of labor-management conflict)

1. List the six issues or sources of conflict between labor and
   management.  Briefly discuss the nature of each one.

   a.

   b.

   c.

   d.

   e.

   f.

2. Describe the general nature of labor-management relations prior to
   the 1930s.  Give examples of how the legal environment prior to the
   1930s was hostile to unionization.

3. Appraise the future prospects for the union movement in the United
   States.

EXERCISE 7-3

(To involve yourself in contemporary business)

1.  Interview a person who is a member of a labor union.  On a separate
    piece of paper, write his or her responses to the following ques-
    tions:

    a.  What are the major goals and roles of unions in the U.S. today?

    b.  What are the major problems confronting unions?

    c.  How can union membership be increased?


2.  Does your state have a right-to-work law?  If so, when was it
    passed?  If not, do you think your state should have such a law?
    Why or why not?


3.  "Unions are no longer a potent political and economic force in the
    U.S."  Do you agree or disagree?  Why?

EXERCISE 7-4

(Puzzle Review)

Arranged in a column below is one of the key concepts from this chapter. Opposite each letter of this key concept is the definition of another key concept also found in this chapter. Fill in the blanks provided with the remaining letters of the defined key concept.

B _ _ _ _ _ _          1.  Union attempt to get people not to deal with a firm

_ _ A _ _              2.  Type of union organized for members of a skilled trade

R _ _ _ _ _ _ _ _ _    3.  Type of law which outlaws the union shop

_ _ G _ _ _  _ _ _     4.  Law often called labor's *Magna Charta*

_ _ _ _ _ A _ _ _      5.  Clause in labor contract granting "cost-of-living" increases in wages

_ _ _ I _ _ _ _ _      6.  In a labor dispute, a third party suggests a possible compromise

_ N _ _ _ _ _ _ _ _    7.  A court order often used by employers in the early days of unions

_ _ _ A _  _ _ _ _ _   8.  The basic union organization

B _ _ _ _ _ _ _        9.  Circulated among employers, naming workers known to favor unions

L _ _ _ _ _ _          10. Employees are denied access to their place of employment by employer

_ _ E _ _ _  _ _ _ _   11. All employees for whom the union bargains must pay dues but need not join

_ _ _ _ I _ _ _ _ _ _  12. In a labor dispute, third party tries to keep negotiations from breaking down

_ _ _ _ S _ _ _         13. Employees need not join unions or pay dues

_ _ _ S _ _ _ _ _ _        14. Only members of union can be hired by employer

_ _ _ _ _ U _ - _ _ _ _ _ _ _       15. 1959 law requiring unions and employers to file reports with Secretary of Labor

_ _ _ _ E _ _ _ _ _        16. Bargaining between unions and employers

S _ _ _ _ _        17. Temporary withdrawal of employees from an employer's service

EXERCISE 7-5

(Incident: The U.S. Supreme Court and Right-to-work laws)

Answer the questions on a plain piece of paper.


Twenty states have right-to-work laws that outlaw the union shop type of union security. (See Figure 7-4 on text page 204). In July 1982, however, the U.S. Supreme Court upheld a lower court finding that a state cannot enforce its right-to-work law on federal enclaves.

A federal enclave is a federally controlled area within a state's borders. For example, the Cape Canaveral Air Force Station in Florida is a federal enclave. Although Florida has a right-to-work law, it cannot enforce the law on the federal enclave. Thus contractors who do work at the site and the unions that represent their employees can have a union shop agreement.


Questions

1. Why do twenty states have right-to-work laws?

2. Why do thirty states not have right-to-work laws?

3. Do you think that the U.S. Supreme Court should have upheld the lower court's ruling? Why or why not?

Test Your Business
Vocabulary

1. H (p. 194)       7. K (pp. 205-206)
2. N (p. 195)       8. D (p. 205)
3. C (p. 196)       9. Q (pp. 212-213)
4. I (p. 200)      10. L (p. 207)
5. P (p. 200)      11. A (p. 213)
6. G (p. 205)      12. J (p. 215)

Programmed Review
(refer to the indicated pages
in the text)

1.                      6.
   A. (p. 195)             A. (pp. 206-211)
   B. (p. 195)             B. (pp. 210-211)
2.                      7.
   A. (p. 196)             A. (p. 212)
   B. (p. 198)             B. (pp. 212-213)
   C. (p. 196)             C. (p. 213)
3.                      8.
   A. (p. 199)             A. (p. 214)
   B. (p. 200)             B. (p. 216)
   C. (p. 200)          9.
4.                         A. (p. 217)
   A. (p. 202)             B. (p. 216)
   B. (p. 201)
5.
   A. (p. 205)
   B. (p. 205)
   C. (p. 202)

Exercise 7-1   (p. 197)

1. D      6. D      11. D
2. A      7. D      12. D
3. B      8. B      13. E
4. C      9. C      14. D
5. A     10. E

Exercise 7-4

1. boycott (p. 215)
2. craft (p. 200)
3. right-to-work (p. 205)
4. Wagner Act (pp. 196-197)
5. escalator (pp. 210-211)
6. mediation (pp. 212-213)
7. injunction (p. 196)
8. local union (p. 200)
9. blacklist (p
10. lockout (p. 216)
11. agency shop (pp. 205-206)
12. conciliation (p. 212)
13. open shop (p. 205)
14. closed shop (p. 205)
15. Landrum-Griffin (p. 198)
16. collective (p. 194)
17. strike (p. 215)

Test Yourself (Multiple Choice

1. D (p. 200)
2. B (pp. 205-206)
3. C (p. 213)
4. A (p. 198)
5. C (p. 207)
6. A (p. 208)
7. C (pp. 210-211)
8. D (p. 216)
9. B (p. 215)
10. D (p. 215)

Test Yourself (True-False)

1. True (P. 205)
2. False (p. 198)
3. False (pp. 212-213)
4. True (p. 215)
5. False (p. 215)
6. True (p. 205)
7. True (p. 194)
8. True (p. 213)
9. False (p. 214)
10. False (p. 195)

# CHAPTER 8

# Production Management

Chapter 8 begins by defining production. Production activity creates goods and services. The production process starts with inputs such as materials, capital goods, and human input. The various ways of classifying production processes include uses of material, timing, and labor use. The outputs of the production process are consumer and industrial goods and services.

The next major section relates the traditional management functions of planning, organizing, staffing, directing, and controlling to the production area. Managers plan the product and the location of the plant. The plant can be organized around a process or a product, depending on the number of products and the volume of production. In addition to organizing, staffing and directing of the production operation must take place. They represent the application of the human resource to the production process. The final function of controlling involves setting production standards and developing systems for comparing production standards.

The production process requires numerous items as inputs. These inputs must be managed and this effort is called materials management. Effective purchasing is an integral part of the materials management process. Through efficient purchasing, the profitability of the firm can be increased.

The final segment of this chapter compares operations management to production management. Operations management is an expanded version of the idea of production management. It represents a systems approach to all business functions with an emphasis on current operations.

# TEST YOUR BUSINESS VOCABULARY

Test your business vocabulary by matching each key concept with the proper phrase. Check your answers with those at the end of this chapter.

## Key Concepts

_____ 1. production
_____ 2. breaking down
_____ 3. intermittent production
_____ 4. continuous production
_____ 5. plant capacity
_____ 6. PERT

_____ 7. reciprocity
_____ 8. value analysis
_____ 9. operations management
_____ 10. combination
_____ 11. obsolescence
_____ 12. capital-intensive

## Phrases

A. Capital investment is a major part of production costs
B. A process for performing repeated tasks in production in which little human supervision is needed
C. A production process that involves removing or separating some of the original input
D. Applies to technological or fashion products
E. The application of the functions of management to a production process
F. An activity that results in the creation of goods and services
G. Emphasis is on the treatment of production, finance, and marketing as parts of a system subject to improvement by scientific management methods
H. The internal design of a factory
I. The limits of the output of a production facility
J. A planning and control tool used by managers to estimate the time needed to complete a project
K. The inspection and/or replacement of certain critical machines to avoid downtime
L. Production carried out routinely and without interruption
M. A production process that involves bringing things together into a new arrangement
N. Production that stops and starts
O. Two firms agree to supply each other
P. The identification of costs and the attempt to cut them where possible
Q. An approach to evaluation of potential suppliers

PROGRAMMED REVIEW

(To help you in understanding the chapter material and to see if you have mastered the objectives stated at the beginning of the chapter)

1. *Illustrate the nature and growth of production.*

    A. Production activity creates _____ and _____.

    B. Production activity starts with the _____ of resources which are fed into one of several kinds of production _____.

2. *Illustrate the inputs, processes, and outputs of production.*

    A. The basic inputs to the production process are _____,

    _____ _____, and _____ _____.

    B. Production processes can be classified according to _____

    _____, _____, and _____.

    C. Outputs of production are divided into _____ and _____ goods and services.

3. *Show how production processes may be classified.*

    A. The two basic time dimensions used for classifying production

    processes are _____ and _____.

    B. The two types of production processes based on the amount of

    human input are _____-intensive and _____- intensive.

4. *Review the management functions and give an example of each as applied to production.*

    A. Production management is the _____ of managerial functions to production.

    B. Production _____ requires a forecast or demand and has short-run and long-run dimensions.

    C. A plant may be arranged according to _____ or according to

    _____, depending on the number of products being produced and the volume of production.

    D. _____ and _____ together represent the application of the human resource to the production process.

101

5. *Develop a checklist for plant location decisions.*

   A. The three important questions that relate to planning for the plant itself are _____

   _____

   _____

   B. Input and _____ transportation costs must be considered in selecting an area for a plant.

6. *Evaluate the dangers of loss of human motivation in a big factory.*

   A. It is easier to _____ workers to outproduce coworkers than to _____ them to operate at the pace dictated by a machine.

   B. It takes _____ to prepare for a change to automation.

7. *Explain the process of control as it applies to product quality.*

   A. When firms inspect and/or replace certain critical machines and parts on a regular basis to avoid downtime, this is called

   _____ maintenance.

   B. A _____ _____ system sets up a standard for an input or output and makes comparisons against this standard.

8. *Distinguish between value analysis and vendor analysis.*

   A. In _____ analysis attention is focused on identifying and eliminating nonessential cost factors.

   B. _____ analysis evaluates the technical, financial, and managerial abilities of potential suppliers.

9. *Distinguish between a production management view and an operations management view of problem solving.*

   A. _____ management represents a systems approach to all business functions.

   B. Operations management emphasizes _____ operations and control rather than long-range planning.

TEST YOURSELF (Multiple Choice)

Test yourself by selecting the best answer.  Check your answers with those at the end of this chapter.

1.  Reciprocity as a purchasing policy means:

    A.  a special discount to regular customers
    B.  shared computer services
    C.  procurement procedures
    D.  two firms agree to supply each other

2.  Which of the following is <u>not</u> a method of classifying production processes?

    A.  uses of material inputs
    B.  product demand
    C.  timing
    D.  labor usage

3.  The limit of the production output of a facility is known as:

    A.  plant layout
    B.  economies of scale
    C.  plant capacity
    D.  expansion point

4.  The process of focusing attention on the identification and elimination of nonessential cost factors is called:

    A.  value analysis
    B.  vendor analysis
    C.  make or buy analysis
    D.  procurement analysis

5.  Operations management represents:

    A.  a narrow viewpoint of business operations
    B.  a systems approach to all business functions
    C.  a production-oriented approach to business
    D.  an approach that focuses on long-range planning

6.  The purchasing function in most modern firms:

    A.  has been eliminated in favor of a decentralized acquisitions function
    B.  seldom practices reciprocity in dealing with suppliers
    C.  is being handled increasingly in a centralized manner
    D.  is seldom subject to policy standardization

7.  Which of the following incorrectly describes production activity?

A. it creates goods and services
B. it helps to satisfy wants
C. it can be viewed as a sequence
D. it is the same as marketing activity

8. Forming a part out of a basic material is called:

A. jobbing
B. intermittent production
C. fabrication
D. production planning

9. Which of the following is <u>not</u> a type of production control?

A. order control
B. product quality control
C. inventory control
D. market demand control

10. A device which shows the standard set of steps to be taken in the performance of a procedure is:

A. a PERT chart
B. a CPM diagram
C. a control chart
D. a quality control system

TEST YOURSELF (True-False)

Test yourself by answering whether the following statements are true or false. Check your answers with those at the end of this chapter.

____ 1. Treatment is doing something to an input without adding or subtracting from it.

____ 2. Usually with the continuous production process, little human supervision is needed.

____ 3. The specific organization for production in a firm should not be influenced by the nature of the production process.

____ 4. Most continuous production processes produce goods to order.

____ 5. Obsolescence is of more concern when dealing with technological or fashion products.

____ 6. If a supplier offers a cumulative quantity discount, it will probably increase the average size of orders.

_____ 7. The process of value analysis may involve a committee including engineers, cost accountants, production representatives, and others.

_____ 8. Output transportation cost depends on the expected location and density of customers in the proposed area.

_____ 9. Quality control means that quality must be consistently high.

_____ 10. Control charts show the standard set of steps to be taken in the performance of a procedure.

EXERCISE 8-1

(To improve your understanding of production inputs and processes)

1.  Under each method of classifying production processes, list and define each of the sub-elements:

    a.  uses of material

        (i)

        (ii)

        (iii)

    b.  timing

        (i)

        (ii)

    c.  labor use

        (i)

        (ii)

2.  List the four categories of human input:

    a.

    b.

    c.

    d.

3.  Classify the following as an intermittent or a continuous production process:

    a.  a cola bottling plant

    b.  a furniture manufacturer that produces painted and unpainted furniture

    c.  a customized stereo system producer

    d.  a manufacturer of paper towels

4. Classify the following as labor-intensive or capital-intensive production processes:

    a.   producing hand-crafted furniture

    b.   producing steel

    c.   refining petroleum

    d.   making mink coats

EXERCISE 8-2

(To improve your understanding of the differences between production and operations management)

1.  What is production management?


2.  Describe below each of the managerial functions as they apply to production management.

    a.  planning

    b.  organizing

    c.  controlling


3.  Define, in your own words, operations management.


4.  From an operations management view, sequentially name the key decisions in the life of a productive system.  The first and final decisions are provided to facilitate the process.

    a.  Birth

    b.  _____  _____ and _____  _____

    c.  _____

    d.  _____

    e.  _____

    f.  _____  _____

    g.  _____

    h.  Termination

EXERCISE 8-3

(To help you understand the importance of plant location decisions and purchasing decisions)

1. Answer on a plain piece of paper.

   A manufacturer of small electrical appliances (toasters, electric blankets, bun warmers, food processors, and coffee makers) is facing the decision of where to locate a new plant. The firm engages basically in a continuous production process that is labor-intensive. It produces some products for sale under the brand name of Montgomery Ward, but roughly 80 percent of its output is sold under the firm's own brand. Thus, it engages in production to order (Montgomery Ward) and production for stock.

   Assume you are on the company committee that is responsible for selecting an area and site for the new plant. Select a city in your state that you think is most favorable to the company and prepare a report that discusses the factors listed in Table 8-1 on page 233 of the text.

2. What is role of purchasing in the organization?

3. What is the basic rationale behind centralized purchasing?

4. Describe the following terms as they relate to purchasing.

   a. reciprocity

   b. vendor analysis

   c. value analysis

   d. make-or-buy decisions

   e. cumulative quantity discount

EXERCISE 8-4

(Review of production terms - crossword puzzle)

## Across

1. Two words that describe the term *plant capacity*
4. _____ analysis often involves the use of a rating system to determine the "best" suppliers
6. Creates products and services
7. Production process of bringing things together
10. "You buy from me and I'll buy from you"
12. Production decision to _____ _____ buy

## Down

1. Inventories are subject to this
2. Plant _____ is the term that describes the arrangement of machines and internal design of a factory
3. Painting or polishing is an example of this production process
5. Preventive maintenance helps to avoid this

13. A word that describes the breaking-down process
14. Production without inter-ruption
16. _____ sampling is a form of production quality control
17. _____ analysis seeks to cut costs by reviewing pro-duct specifications

8. Noncontinuous type of production process
9. A _____ chart aids in the scheduling of production
11. _____ -intensive describes the productive process that is mainly dependent on machinery, plant, and equipment
15. The opposite of happy

EXERCISE 8-5

(Return of the Convertible)

Answer the questions on a plain piece of paper.

What was supposed to be the last mass produced convertible car in the United States was manufactured in 1976 by Cadillac. Thereafter, people who wanted convertibles would have to buy conventional hardtop cars and have them converted by independent body shops. American automobile manufacturers felt that the demand for convertibles was insufficient to justify devoting an entire assembly line to produce a small number of cars.

Independent body shops, called customizers, enjoyed a big boom in business in the years immediately after 1976. Apparently, thousands of convertible lovers were willing to pay the relatively high cost of converting their conventional cars to convertibles. Thus, in 1982, Chrysler signed contracts with Cars & Concepts Inc. to convert some units of the Le Baron.

The convertible reached the high point of its popularity during the 1960s. But unlike cars built then, modern cars are built without frames, and they rely on welded sheet metal to provide structural rigidity. More support must be added when there is no roof. Thus, Chrysler builds in the extra support along with the roofs. Then it sends the cars to Cars & Concepts where the roof is removed. Chrysler figures the cost of adapting its assembly line to skip the roofs would be too high.

Questions

1.  Is Chrysler's production process one of combination, breaking down, or treatment? What about that used by Cars & Concepts? Explain your answers.

2.  Do traditional car customizers produce for stock? What about the contracts between Chrysler and Cars & Concepts? Do you think they involve production for stock? Explain your answers.

3.  Was there a "make-or-buy" decision involved in the Chrysler and Cars & Concepts arrangement? Explain.

Test your Business
Vocabulary

1. F (p. 224)     7. O (p. 247)
2. C (p. 226)     8. P (p. 247)
3. N (p. 227)     9. G (p. 248)
4. L (p. 227)    10. M (p. 226)
5. I (p. 235)    11. D (p. 244)
6. J (p. 241)    12. A (p. 228)

Programmed Review
(refer to the indicated pages
in the text)

1.                   5.
  A. (p. 224)          A. (p. 232)
  B. (p. 224)          B. (p. 233)
2.                   6.
  A. (p. 224)          A. (p. 238)
  B. (p. 225)          B. (p. 238)
  C. (p. 229)        7.
3.                     A. (p. 243)
  A. (p. 227)          B. (p. 242)
  B. (p. 228)        8.
4.                     A. (p. 247)
  A. (p. 231)          B. (p. 247)
  B. (p. 231)        9.
  C. (p. 236)          A. (p. 248)
  D. (p. 238)          B. (p. 248)

Test Yourself (Multiple Choice)

 1. D (p. 247)
 2. B (p. 225)
 3. C (p. 235)
 4. A (p. 247)
 5. B (p. 248)
 6. C (p. 245)
 7. D (p. 224)
 8. C (p. 226)
 9. D (p. 239)
10. C (p. 239)

Test Yourself (True-False)

1. True (p. 226)    6. False (p. 246)
2. True (p. 227)    7. True (p. 247)
3. False (p. 237)   8. True (p. 233)
4. False (p. 227)   9. False (p. 242)
5. True (p. 244)   10. True (p. 239)

Exercise 8-1

1A. combination, breaking
    down, and treatment (p.
    225)
1B. intermittent and contin-
    uous (p.227)
1C. labor-intensive and
    capital-intensive
2.  a. unskilled labor
    b. skilled labor
    c. supervisory skills
    d. managerial skills
          (p. 225)
3.  a and d continuous; b and
    c intermittent (p. 227)
4.  b and c capital-intensive;
    a and d labor-intensive
    (p. 228)

Exercise 8-4

1. (across) output limit
   (p. 235)
1. (down) obsolescence
   (p. 244)
2. layout (p. 235)
3. treatment (p. 226)
4. vendor (p. 247)
5. downtime (p. 243)
6. production (p. 224)
7. combination (p. 226)
8. intermittent (p. 227)
9. control (p. 239)
10. reciprocity (p. 247)
11. capital (p. 228)
12. make or (p. 232)
13. separation (p. 226)
14. continuous (p. 227)
15. sad
16. acceptance (p. 243)
17. value (p. 247)

# CHAPTER 9

# The Marketing Concept

Chapter 9 is the first chapter concerning marketing. It describes the nature of marketing and its role in the organization. Marketing is the entire group of activities undertaken to find, influence, and serve customers for goods and services. Marketing, along with other functional areas, is guided philosophically by the marketing concept. It means that the whole firm is coordinated to achieve one goal - to serve its present and potential customers and to do so at a profit.

In order to implement the marketing concept, target markets must be defined. This is the set of customers to whom marketing efforts are directed. Markets may be industrial or consumer. Industrial markets are firms or institutions, while consumer markets are usually ultimate household consumers. Goods and services may also be classified as consumer or industrial.

Firms may pursue alternative marketing strategies such as product differentiation and market segmentation. Product differentiation tries to convince target customers that one brand is different from the competition's. Market segmentation calls for making a special marketing mix for a special segment of the market.

The next section deals with marketing research. If marketing managers are to make sound decisions, marketing research must be conducted. This research may take one of two basic approaches - demographic or behavioral. Both approaches provide essential information for decision-making.

In conclusion, the chapter provides an overview of marketing fundamentals. This overview serves as a foundation for the next sections covering product, promotion, distribution, and pricing considerations.

# TEST YOUR BUSINESS VOCABULARY

Test your business vocabulary by matching each key concept with the proper phrase. Check your answers with those at the end of this chapter.

## Key Concepts

___ 1. marketing
___ 2. marketing concept
___ 3. target market
___ 4. product differentiation
___ 5. market segmentation
___ 6. form utility
___ 7. time utility

___ 8. primary research
___ 9. secondary research
___ 10. focus group interview
___ 11. convenience goods
___ 12. shopping goods
___ 13. industrial goods
___ 14. middlemen

## Phrases

A. Items that are habitually purchased
B. Product sold to business firms
C. The buyer will make a great effort to locate and purchase the specific brand
D. Achieving goals by providing customer satisfaction at a profit to the firm
E. Gathering new facts for a specific purpose
F. The systematic gathering, recording, and analyzing of data concerning the marketing of goods and services
G. Firms that participate in buying and selling products as part of a channel of distribution
H. Usefulness because of shape or arrangement of parts
I. Includes product design, place, promotion, and pricing activities
J. Consumer products whose purchase is taken seriously enough to require comparison and study
K. The increase in value resulting from the passage of time
L. The actual transfer of title to a product creates this type of utility
M. Libraries are a frequent source for this kind of research
N. Designing a special marketing mix for a special group
O. A marketing research tool
P. The set of customers to which a firm directs its efforts
Q. This type of research collects facts about people, families, or firms who are likely to become customers
R. A process of convincing target customers that one brand is distinct from and better than the competition's

# PROGRAMMED REVIEW

(To help you in understanding the chapter material and to see if you have mastered the objectives stated at the beginning of the chapter)

1. *Discuss the nature of marketing.*

   A. Marketing is the whole set of activities undertaken to

      _____, _____, and _____ customers for products
      and services.

   B. Marketing may involve creating or _____ new wants.

2. *Demonstrate the relationship between income level and discretionary
   income.*

   A. What a buyer has to spend on things other than _____ is
      called discretionary income.

   B. The more income a family or person has, the smaller is the

      _____ of income required for absolute necessities.

3. *Explain the consumer's role in the marketing concept.*

   A. The goal of the marketing concept is to serve present and

      _____ customers at a _____ to the firm.

   B. If a firm is to provide customer satisfaction in a profitable

      way it must operate as a well-coordinated _____.

4. *Give examples of industrial and household target markets.*

   A. If a firm is to adopt the marketing concept, it must define the

      _____ of its customers.

   B. _____ goods and services are used by firms or institutions
      to make other products or to provide services.

5. *Compare the strategies of differentiation and segmentation.*

   A. _____ _____ is a process of convincing target cus-
      tomers that one brand is different from, and better than, the
      competition's.

   B. _____ _____ calls for making a special marketing
      mix for a special segment of the market.

6. *Name and explain two different approaches to marketing research.*

   A. Two general approaches to the study of the market are the
      _____ approach and the _____ approach.

B. Looking things up in already-available materials is called
_____ research.

C. The _____ approach asks the question "Why consumers buy?"

7. *Distinguish among four kinds of utility in a product.*

A. The four types of utility are _____, _____, _____,

and _____.

B. _____ utility is determined by location.

8. *Discuss the history and effects of consumerism.*

A. Consumerism is a movement to strengthen the power of _____
in relation to the power of _____.

B. Many of the consumer laws give protection in the areas of

_____,_____ _____, and information on consumer
financing plans.


TEST YOURSELF (Multiple Choice)

Test yourself by selecting the best answer. Check your answers with
those at the end of this chapter.

1. The type of research that focuses on the collection of facts about
people, families, or firms that are thought likely to become
customers is called:

A. primary research
B. demographic research
C. secondary research
D. behavioral research

2. A manufacturer of a convenience good:

A. advertises in publications of limited circulation
B. uses detailed, rational advertising
C. seeks wide distribution
D. does not advertise much

3. Which of the following activities is not usually considered part
of the domain of marketing?

A. transportation
B. retailing
C. sales force management
D. quality control

117

4. The amount of income that buyers have to spend after they have paid for necessities is called:

   A. discretionary income
   B. disposable income
   C. complementary income
   D. aggregate income

5. Goods for which strong conviction as to brand, style, or type already exists in the buyer's mind are called:

   A. shopping goods
   B. specialty goods
   C. convenience goods
   D. frequently-sought goods

6. Which one of the following statements is inconsistent with the philosophy of market segmentation?

   A. Market segmentation calls for making a special marketing mix for a special segment.
   B. There is more than one set of needs to be satisfied within the general market.
   C. Market segmentation treats customers as one general target group to be aimed at with one common marketing mix.
   D. Market segmentation may be based on demographic and behavioral factors.

7. The principle of diminishing marginal utility is most closely associated with the creation of:

   A. time utility
   B. form utility
   C. place utility
   D. ownership utility

8. Which one of the following is not a characteristic of the industrial market?

   A. The target market is generally smaller than it is for consumer products.
   B. Industrial customers are often less concentrated geographically than household consumers.
   C. Industrial buyers usually have more formal systems for buying than household consumers.
   D. Industrial marketers practice market segmentation.

9. Which of the following is an example of primary research?

   A. using U.S. Census publications
   B. using U.S. Department of Labor statistics

C. using local sales tax figures

D. distributing questionnaires to college students asking about their use of leisure time

10. The set of activities which marketers use to go along with the product or service is called:

    A. product mix
  ' B. promotional mix
    C. marketing mix
    D. planning mix

TEST YOURSELF (True-False)

Test yourself by answering whether the following statements are true or false. Check your answers with those at the end of the chapter.

___ 1. Marketing sometimes involves creating something or stimulating new wants.

___ 2. A strategy of product differentiation treats customers as one general target group.

___ 3. When considering the industrial area the target market is generally larger than it is for consumer products.

___ 4. Most clothing, appliances, and cars fall into the category of shopping goods.

___ 5. The demographic approach to market research seeks to understand why buyers feel and behave the way they do.

___ 6. Secondary research is always of more value than primary research.

___ 7. Focus group interviews provide stimulating ideas for further research.

___ 8. Consumerism is a movement started in the early 1900s by the federal government to reduce the power of American corporations.

___ 9. Ownership utility is related to the passage of legal title to the final user.

___ 10. Retailers and wholesalers are examples of middlemen.

EXERCISE 9-1

(To improve your understanding of product differentiation and market segmentation)

1.  Define the following terms and give examples:

    a.  product differentiation

    b.  market segmentation

2.  Is it possible for market planners to focus on only one segment of a market?  Explain.

3.  List six bases for segmenting markets.

    a.

    b.

    c.

    d.

    e.

    f.

4.  How can the construction of a grid help marketing managers make
    segmentation decisions?

EXERCISE 9-2

(To improve your understanding of the differences between consumer and industrial markets)

1. Define the following terms and give examples of each.

   A.  consumer good

   B.  industrial good

2. List the categories of consumer and industrial goods.

   A.  consumer goods

      a)

      b)

      c)

   B.  industrial goods

      a)

      b)

      c)

      d)

      e)

      f)

3. Characterize governmental and institutional markets.

EXERCISE 9-3

(To strengthen your understanding of the concept of utility)

1.  List and define the four type of utility.

    a.

    b.

    c.

    d.

2.  Explain how the four utilities are created for an automobile.

3.  "Middlemen do not create anything.  They merely resell products that
    have been produced by manufacturers."  Do you agree?  Why or why not?

4.  Complete the following table.

CLASSES OF CONSUMER GOODS

|  | Convenience | Shopping | Specialty |
|---|---|---|---|
| How far will a buyer travel? | _____ | _____ | _____ |
| How much does it cost? | _____ | _____ | _____ |
| How often purchased? | _____ | _____ | _____ |
| Emphasis on comparison? | _____ | _____ | _____ |
| Purchased habitually? | _____ | _____ | _____ |
| Which advertising media? | _____ | _____ | _____ |

EXERCISE 9-4

(Word Puzzle)

Arranged in a column below is one of the key concepts from this chapter. Opposite each letter of this key concept is the definition or description of another important term used in the chapter, although not necessarily a key concept. Fill in the blanks provided with the remaining letters of the appropriate term.

_ _ _ _ _ _ M _ _ _ _ _

1. The group to whom marketers focus their efforts.

_ _ A _ _ _ _ _ _ _ _ _

2. It is determined by location.

_ _ _ _ _ _ _ _ _ _ _ R _ _ _ _ _ _ _ _

3. Convincing target customers that one brand is better than others.

_ _ _ K _ _ _ _ _ _ _ _ _ _ _

4. To serve present and potential customers at a profit.

_ _ _ _ _ E _ _ _

5. Retailers and wholesalers are examples.

T _ _ _ _ _ _ _ _ _ _

6. Determined by the passage of time.

I _ _ _ _ _ _ _ _ _ _ _ _ _ _

7. Goods used by a firm to make another product.

_ _ N _ _ _ _ _ _ _ _ _ _ _ _

8. Related to the passage of legal title to the final user.

_ _ _ _ _ _ _ _ G _ _ _ _

9. Buyers have strong conviction as to brand and style.

EXERCISE 9-5

(Incident: WATS as a Marketing Tool)

Answer the questions on a plain piece of paper.

Procter & Gamble, Polaroid, Whirlpool, and a growing number of other marketers are using WATS (wide area telecommunications service) numbers as part of their marketing strategy. Target customers who want to ask questions about how to use products or where to get them repaired, to register complaints, and so on, can call 1-800 toll-free telephone numbers and talk to company representatives. Typically, the toll-free numbers are included on or inside product packages.

Questions:

1. Would a firm that is implementing the marketing concept be likely to use the tool described above? Why or why not?

2. Does the WATS line have any potential value to firms that sell industrial goods? Why or why not?

3. Can the tool help a marketer to implement a strategy of product differentiation? Explain.

4. How might the tool help marketers in conducting marketing research?

5. How is the tool related to consumerism?

Test Your Business
Vocabulary

| | |
|---|---|
| 1. I (p. 260) | 8. E (p. 277) |
| 2. D (p. 262) | 9. M (p. 276) |
| 3. P (p. 263) | 10. O (p. 279) |
| 4. R (p. 271) | 11. A (p. 268) |
| 5. N (p. 271) | 12. J (p. 268) |
| 6. H (p. 279) | 13. B (p. 263) |
| 7. K (p. 280) | 14. G (p. 263) |

Programmed Review
(refer to the indicated pages
in the text)

1.
   A. (p. 260)
   B. (p. 260)
2.
   A. (p. 261)
   B. (p. 261)
3.
   A. (p. 262)
   B. (p. 262)
4.
   A. (p. 263)
   B. (p. 263)
5.
   A. (p. 271)
   B. (p. 271)
6.
   A. (p. 276)
   B. (p. 276)
   C. (p. 278)
7.
   A. (p. 279)
   B. (pp. 279-280)
8.
   A. (p. 280)
   B. (p. 281)

Test Yourself (Multiple Choice)

| | |
|---|---|
| 1. B (p. 276) | 6. C (p. 271) |
| 2. C (p. 270) | 7. A (p. 280) |
| 3. D (p. 260) | 8. B (pp. 263-264) |
| 4. A (p. 261) | 9. D (p. 277) |
| 5. B (p. 269) | 10. C (p. 270) |

Test Yourself (True-False)

1. True (p. 260)
2. True (p. 271)
3. False (pp. 263-265)
4. True (pp. 268-269)
5. False (p. 276)
6. False (p. 276)
7. True (p. 279)
8. False (p. 280)
9. True (p. 280)
10. True (p. 263)

Exercise 9-2

1A and 1B (p. 263)
2A (p. 268)
2B (p. 264)
3 (p. 265)

Exercise 9-4

1. target market (p. 263)
2. place utility (pp. 279-280)
3. product differentiation
                    (p. 271)
4. marketing concept (p. 262)
5. middlemen (p. 263)
6. time utility (p. 280)
7. industrial goods (p. 263)
8. ownership utility (p. 280)
9. specialty goods (p. 269)

# CHAPTER 10

# The Product and Its Distribution

Chapter 10 builds on the foundation presented in the last chapter. In an attempt to implement the marketing concept firms must pay particular attention to product, distribution, promotion and pricing considerations. These elements comprise the marketing mix. The focus of this chapter is the product and its distribution.

The product can be defined as a "bundle of satisfactions" which includes the brand, the package, and the services that go with it. During its life cycle, a product may go through the introduction, growth, maturity, and decline phases. The challenge for marketing is to manage properly the elements of the marketing mix through the duration of the cycle. In addition to managing the life cycle, marketers must also manage the product mix. This is the combination of products a firm produces and sells.

The last half of the chapter concentrates on distribution, which is concerned with the movement of products through a channel from producer to user. Members of the channel of distribution provide essential services depending on their type and nature. Merchant middlemen take title to the products they offer for sale, while agent middlemen do not.

The final section discusses physical distribution. The objective here is to minimize total costs without sacrificing the desired level of customer service. The major modes of transportation, such as railroads, trucking, waterways, airlines, and pipelines facilitate the achievement of a firm's physical distribution objectives.

# TEST YOUR BUSINESS VOCABULARY

Test your business vocabulary by matching each key concept with the proper phrase. Check your answers with those at the end of this chapter.

## Key Concepts

____ 1. marketing mix
____ 2. product
____ 3. product life cycle
____ 4. planned obsolescence
____ 5. product mix
____ 6. brand
____ 7. patent
____ 8. trademark
____ 9. place (or distribution)
____ 10. channel of distribution
____ 11. manufacturers' agent
____ 12. physical distribution
____ 13. total cost concept
____ 14. common carrier
____ 15. contract carrier

## Phrases

A. The set of firms directly involved in selling a product
B. It simplifies handling at points of transfer, loading, and unloading
C. Product, price, promotion, and place
D. Makes temporary agreements with individual shippers to move their freight
E. A name, term, symbol, or design, or a combination of them used to identify the goods or services of a seller
F. Examples include car dealerships and fast-food restaurants
G. Protects against imitation for 17 years
H. Introduction, growth, maturity, decline/obsolescence
I. It includes the package, brand, and physical characteristics
J. Offers its services to the general public at uniform rates
K. An agent middleman
L. All products offered for sale by a firm
M. A legally protected name or symbol
N. Intentionally scheduled replacement of a previous product or model
O. Advertising, personal selling, sales promotion, and publicity
P. An approach to viewing all factors that may influence the amount spent on physical distribution
Q. Also called logistics
R. An element of the marketing mix concerned with the movement of products through a channel from producer to consumer
S. The single most important factor in marketing

PROGRAMMED REVIEW

(To help you in understanding the chapter material and to see if you
have mastered the objectives stated at the beginning of the chapter)

1. *Describe the components of a firm's marketing mix.*

   A. The four elements of the marketing mix are _____,

      _____, _____, and _____.

   B. The elements of the marketing mix are focused on _____ and

      _____ customers and are influenced by environmental factors.

2. *Construct a chart showing how the four "Ps" relate to the target
   market and to the environment.*

   A. Some of the environmental factors that marketers must consider

      are _____, _____, _____, and _____.

   B. The _____ element is the key element in the marketing mix
      for cars.

3. *Identify the bundle of satisfactions offered by a product to its
   user.*

   A. The bundle of satisfactions might include the _____,

      _____, _____ and the services that go with it.

   B. Decisions about what and how much to produce represent the
      first step in the _____ planning process.

4. *Draw a chart illustrating the life cycle of a product.*

   A. The four phases of the product life cycle are _____,

      _____, _____, and _____.

   B. Sales volume begins to level off and decline in the _____
      stage of the life cycle.

5. *Present arguments for and against a broad product mix.*

   A. A manufacturer's or a retailer's _____ is the
      combination of products it produces or sells.

   B. A firm with a _____ product mix has a kind of insurance
      against the dangers of obsolescence.

C. A firm that has a _____ product mix also tends to have a lot of depth.

6. *Explain the functions that a package performs.*

   A. The functions of packaging are _____

   _____

   _____

   _____.

   B. The egg carton and the six-pack beverage container illustrate the importance of convenient _____.

7. *Distinguish between brands, patents, and labels.*

   A. Brands usually include both a _____ and a _____.

   B. A _____ protects an invention, a chemical formula, or a new way of doing something from imitation.

   C. The _____ describes the content, nutrition, durability, precautions, and other special product features.

8. *Illustrate how a middleman may bring about economies in distribution.*

   A. The three basic types of middlemen are _____, _____, and _____.

   B. The wholesaler buys in _____ quantities and sells in _____ quantities.

9. *Provide an illustration of the total cost concept.*

   A. Firms try to _____ their total costs without sacrificing their desired level of customer _____.

   B. The objective of modern physical distribution management is to achieve a _____ between costs and service.

10. *Compare the major modes of transportation.*

    A. The five major modes of transportation are _____, _____, _____, _____, and _____.

    B. Piggyback, fishyback, and birdyback are examples of _____ transportation.

TEST YOURSELF (Multiple Choice)

Test yourself by selecting the best answer.  Check your answers with
those at the end of this chapter.

1.  The life history of a product is called:

    A.  the product pattern
    B.  the product line
    C.  the service history
    D.  the product life cycle

2.  A carrier which offers its services to the general public at
    uniform, published rates is a _____ carrier.

    A.  common
    B.  contract
    C.  scheduled
    D.  private

3.  One of these is <u>not</u> an element of the marketing mix.  Which one is
    it?

    A.  product
    B.  place
    C.  planning
    D.  price

4.  Which phase of the product life cycle is usually considered the
    longest?

    A.  introduction
    B.  growth
    C.  maturity
    D.  decline/obsolescence

5.  Piggyback, fishyback, and birdyback are examples of:

    A.  containerization
    B.  intermodal transportation
    C.  agent middlemen
    D.  channels of distribution

6.  The transportation mode which moves the greatest volume of freight
    is:

    A.  the railroad
    B.  the motor truck
    C.  the pipeline
    D.  the waterway

7. Which one of the following is not a type of middleman?

   A.  merchant
   B.  agent
   C.  facilitating
   D.  exchange

8. Brands developed by middlemen are called:

   A.  manufacturers' brands
   B.  national brands
   C.  distributors' or private brands
   D.  local brands

9. Packaging considerations are most closely associated with which one of the marketing mix variables?

   A.  promotion
   B.  product
   C.  price
   D.  place

10. Car dealerships and fast-food restaurants are generally good examples of:

   A.  a franchised retailer
   B.  a non-franchised cooperative
   C.  a manufacturers' agent
   D.  a facilitating agent


TEST YOURSELF (True-Fasle)

Test yourself by answering whether the following statements are true or false.  Check your answers with those at the end of this chapter.

____ 1. Decisions about what and how much to produce represent the first step in the product planning process.

____ 2. A transportation system owned by a manufacturer or middleman for the exclusive use in moving its own products is called a common carrier.

____ 3. Distributors' brands are the same as private brands.

____ 4. The maturity phase of the product life cycle ends when a better product appears or a need disappears and the old product enters the period of decline.

____ 5. Informative labeling of products did not result from consumerism efforts.

___ 6. Merchant middlemen take title to the products that they offer for sale.

___ 7. The major advantage of motor transport is its extreme flexibility.

___ 8. When a product becomes obsolete because its appearance or style has changed, it is technologically obsolete.

___ 9. Patents protect against imitation for 17 years.

___ 10. Containerization increases the complexities of handling products at points of transfer, loading, and unloading.

EXERCISE 10-1

(To improve your understanding of the product element of the marketing mix)

1.  What is a product?

2.  Describe each phase of the product life cycle:

    a.  introduction

    b.  growth

    c.  maturity

    d.  decline/obsolescence

3.  Why is the life cycle of a particular brand shorter than that of the product class?  Give examples.

4.  Define the various types of product obsolescence and give examples:

    a.  planned obsolescence

    b.  technological obsolescence

    c.  fashion obsolescence

5.  Discuss the advantages of broad and narrow product mixes.  Give examples of each.

EXERCISE 10-2

(To improve your understanding of the distribution element of the marketing mix)

1. Channels of distribution functions include the following:

   a. _____

   b. _____

   c. _____

   d. _____

2. The final development of a channel depends on:

   a. _____

   b. _____

   c. _____

   d. _____

3. The three basic types of middlemen are:

   a. _____

   b. _____

   c. _____

4. What are the economic advantages in a system of distribution that uses a wholesaler?

   a. _____

   b. _____

   c. _____

   d. _____

5. What is the objective of physical distribution management? _____

   _____

   _____

EXERCISE 10-3

(To review the main modes of transportation)

1. Indicate whether each of the following pertains to railroads, motor truck, pipelines, ships and barges, or airlines (more than one mode of transportation may apply in some cases).

|  | Railroads | Motor Trucks | Pipelines | Ships and Barges | Airlines |
|---|---|---|---|---|---|
| a. Relatively small capital investment | ___ | ___ | ___ | ___ | ___ |
| b. Economies of scale are quite evident | ___ | ___ | ___ | ___ | ___ |
| c. Accommodate high-value cargo | ___ | ___ | ___ | ___ | ___ |
| d. Involve accessibility problems | ___ | ___ | ___ | ___ | ___ |
| e. Still mainly people-oriented | ___ | ___ | ___ | ___ | ___ |
| f. Most invisible | ___ | ___ | ___ | ___ | ___ |
| g. Most flexible | ___ | ___ | ___ | ___ | ___ |
| h. High incidence of private carriage | ___ | ___ | ___ | ___ | ___ |
| i. Least labor-intensive operation | ___ | ___ | ___ | ___ | ___ |
| j. Least affected by weather | ___ | ___ | ___ | ___ | ___ |

2. What are the advantages of intermodal transportation? Describe the following types of intermodal transportation.

   a.  piggyback

   b.  fishyback

   c.  birdyback

EXERCISE 10-4

(Word Puzzle)

Arranged in a column below is one of the key concepts from this chapter. Opposite each letter of this key concept is the definition or description of another important term used in the chapter, although not necessarily a key concept. Fill in the blanks provided with the remaining letters of the appropriate term.

P _ _ _ _                     1. The same as distribution.

_ R _ _ _                     2. Usually includes both a name and a symbol.

_ O _ _ _ _ _ _ _ _ _ _       3. Offers service to the general public at uniform rates.

D _ _ _ _ _ _ _ _ _ _         4. The same as place.

_ _ _ _ U _ _                 5. A bundle of satisfactions.

C _ _ _ _ _ _ _ _ _ _ _ _ _   6. Preloaded by the seller to move freight.

_ _ _ _ _ T                   7. It protects a new idea for 17 years.

L _ _ _ _                     8. It describes the content of a product.

_ _ _ _ _ _ _ _ I _           9. All products produced by a firm.

F _ _ _ _ _ _ _ _ _ _ _ _ _ _ _ _

                              10. McDonald's is an example.

_ _ _ _ E _ _ _               11. It protects a name or symbol when registered.

138

_ _ _ _ _ _ C _ _ _ _ _ _ _ _       12. Negotiable con-
                                        tracts with
                                        shippers.

_ _ Y _ _ _ _ _ _ _ _ _ _ _ _ _ _ _
                                    13. The same as
                                        logistics.

_ _ _ _ _ C _ _ _ _ _ _ _ _ _       14. It considers all
                                        costs concerned
                                        with distribution.

_ _ _ _ _ _ _ L _ _ _ _ _ _ _ _ _ _ _   15. Products move
                                            through this.

_ _ _ _ _ _ _ _ _ _ E _ _ _ _ _ _ _     16. They are paid
                                            commissions to
                                            represent manu-
                                            facturers.

EXERCISE 10-5

(Incident: Levi Strauss & Co. Changes Its Distribution Strategy)

Answer the questions on a plain piece of paper.


Levi Strauss & Co. traditionally distributed its apparel through department stores and specialty stores. These types of stores, however, have been stocking a greater proportion of designer jeans and other apparel that offer higher profit margins. Thus, they could give less space to Levi products.

Levi Strauss, therefore, recently decided to change its distribution strategy and began distributing through mass merchandisers like Sears and J.C. Penney. This has tended to alienate some of the department stores and specialty stores that still stock some of Levi's products.

Questions

1. What "bundle of satisfactions" might a buyer receive when he or she buys a pair of Levi jeans?

2. Does the product life cycle concept apply to a product that has been around as long as blue jeans? Explain.

3. Do you think Levi jeans (a manufacturer brand) will take sales away from jeans marketed under the Sears and Penney labels in Sears and Penney stores? Why or why not?

4. Why do you think that some of Levi's department store and specialty store accounts were alienated by Levi's decision to distribute through Sears and J.C. Penney?

Test Your Business
Vocabulary

1. C (p. 286)
2. I (p. 288)
3. H (pp. 288-289)
4. N (p. 291)
5. L (p. 293)
6. E (p. 294)
7. G (p. 296)
8. M (p. 296)
9. R (p. 297)
10. A (p. 298)
11. K (p. 299)
12. Q (p. 303)
13. P (p. 303)
14. J (p. 304)
15. D (p. 305)

Programmed Review
(refer to the indicated pages
in the text)

1.
  A. (p. 286)
  B. (p. 286)
2.
  A. (p. 287)
  B. (p. 286)
3.
  A. (p. 288)
  B. (p. 288)
4.
  A. (p. 288)
  B. (p. 290)
5.
  A. (p. 293)
  B. (p. 293)
  C. (p. 294)

6.
  A. (p. 294)
  B. (p. 294)
7.
  A. (p. 294)
  B. (p. 296)
  C. (p. 296)
8.
  A. (p. 299)
  B. (p. 302)
9.
  A. (p. 303)
  B. (p. 303)
10.
  A. (pp. 305-307)
  B. (p. 308)

Test Yourself (Multiple Choice)

1. D (p. 288)
2. A (p. 304)
3. C (p. 286)
4. C (p. 290)
5. B (p. 308)
6. A (pp. 305-306)
7. D (p. 299)
8. C (p. 296)
9. B (p. 294)
10. A (p. 301)

Test Yourself (True-False)

1. True (p. 288)
2. False (p. 304)
3. True (p. 296)
4. True (p. 290)
5. False (p. 296)
6. True (p. 299)
7. True (p. 306)
8. False (pp. 291-292)
9. True (p. 296)
10. False (pp. 307-308)

Exercise 10-3

1. railroads: b,d  (p. 305)
  motor trucks: a,g,h (p. 306)
  pipelines: b,d,f,i,j (p. 306)
  ships and barges: b,d,h
               (p. 306)
  airlines: c,e, (p. 307)

2. (p. 308)

Exercise 10-4

1. place (p. 297)
2. brand (p. 294)
3. common carrier (p. 304)
4. distribution (p. 297)
5. product (p. 288)
6. containerization (pp. 307-308)
7. patent (p. 296)
8. label (p. 296)
9. product mix (p. 293)
10. franchised retailer (p. 301)
11. trademark (p. 296)
12. contract carrier (p. 305)
13. physical distribution (p. 303)
14. total cost concept (p. 303)
15. channel of distribution (p. 298)
16. manufacturers' agent (p. 299)

# CHAPTER 11

# Promotion and Pricing

Chapter 11 provides a continuation of the discussion about the marketing mix. Both promotion and pricing considerations are essential in developing a sound marketing program. Promotion is communication that gains attention, teaches, reminds, persuades, and reassures. The principal methods of promotion are advertising and personal selling. Other methods include sales promotion, publicity, and public relations.

The last half of the chapter focuses on price. The price element includes the dollar cost to customers as well as the conditions of sale. The cost and demand approaches to setting price provide alternative guidelines for marketers. The cost approach involves building unit selling prices on the basis of cost. On the other hand, the demand approach considers possible customer reaction and this approach is more consistent with the marketing concept.

When marketers consider pricing strategies for new products, they usually evaluate market penetration and market skimming. The former features a low initial price in an attempt to build a large market share and to build brand loyalty. The latter features a high initial price in an attempt to get the greatest early revenues from sales to recover product development costs.

The last section explores the area of services marketing. With the rapid increase in services, marketers must focus their efforts on improving the application of the marketing concept to this important area.

# TEST YOUR BUSINESS VOCABULARY

Test your business vocabulary by matching each key concept with the proper phrase. Check your answers with those at the end of this chapter.

## Key Concepts

____ 1. promotion
____ 2. account executive
____ 3. advertising
____ 4. AIDA process
____ 5. personal selling
____ 6. publicity
____ 7. sales promotion
____ 8. oligopoly
____ 9. monopolistic competition
____ 10. markup
____ 11. cash discount
____ 12. market penetration pricing
____ 13. skimming pricing
____ 14. inventory turnover rate
____ 15. functional discount
____ 16. pricing model
____ 17. public relations
____ 18. price lining

## Phrases

A. The process of selling sought by advertising and personal selling
B. An element of the marketing mix which includes monetary cost and the terms of sale
C. An example is an advertising allowance
D. A mathematical formula to help firms set the best basic price
E. Information about a company or its product that is considered "news" by the media
F. A few firms sell highly similar products and dominate a market
G. It includes trading stamps, contests, and special attractions
H. Includes all communication a firm has with its present or potential customers
I. Setting retail prices bought at a variety of wholesale prices to simplify consumer decisions
J. A discount based on the amount bought
K. A market condition where product homogeneity exists
L. An addition to cost by a middleman
M. Coordinates relationship between client and advertising agency
N. A face-to-face sales effort
O. A discount given to middlemen in proportion to their position in the channel of distribution
P. All nonpersonal promotional activity for which a fee is paid by an identified sponsor
Q. Small discounts for prompt payment of bills
R. Many sellers compete for customers by offering differentiated products
S. Communication with the public that seeks to create goodwill
T. A high rate indicates efficiency in the use of resources
U. Setting a high initial price in order to get maximum quick return on product development costs
V. Setting a price low to secure a market share for the product
W. Any means by which advertising can be carried

PROGRAMMED REVIEW

(To help you in understanding the chapter material and to see if you
have mastered the objectives stated at the beginning of the chapter)

1. *Explain the role of promotion.*

   A. Promotion includes all _____ by a firm with its customers
      for the purpose of expanding sales, directly or indirectly.

   B. Promotion is communication that gains attention, teaches,

      _____, _____, and reassures.

2. *Describe the activities of an advertising agency, including media
   selection and printed ad composition.*

   A. Advertising agencies serve clients by _____ advertising
      campaigns, by buying _____ and _____ in the broadcast
      and print media, and by checking that ads appear as agreed.

   B. An _____ _____ is in charge of the entire relation-
      ship between the agency and a particular client.

3. *Summarize public complaints against and regulation of advertising
   in the U.S. in recent years.*

   A. Laws passed by states to control deceptive advertising are

      called _____ _____ statutes.

   B. Some complaints relate to _____ in advertising which
      limits the degree of exaggeration permitted.

4. *Give a brief description of the functions of selling and sales
   management.*

   A. Personal selling includes any _____

      for the purpose of increasing, directly or indirectly, a firm's
      sales.

   B. The sales manager's responsibilities include _____ an

      effective salesforce, _____ the salesforce, and _____

      the sales effort.

5. *Differentiate between publicity, public relations, and sales promotion.*

A.  _____ is a communication through the news media as a legitimate part of the news.

B.  _____ _____ includes any personal communication with the public that seeks to create goodwill for the firm.

C.  _____ _____ includes special events directed at increasing sales.

6.  *Distinguish between two approaches to basic price and illustrate how market conditions influence pricing.*

A.  The _____ approach to setting basic price involves building unit selling prices on the basis of cost.

B.  The _____ approach to pricing is more compatible with the marketing concept.

7.  *Describe two possible pricing strategies for introducing a new product.*

A.  To feature low price when introducing a new product is called _____ _____ pricing.

B.  To feature a high price when introducing a new product is called _____ _____ pricing.

8.  *Provide an illustration of price lining in a retail store.*

A.  Price lining involves _____ the products at three or four sales price levels.

B.  The use of odd pricing occurs partly out of tradition and partly because of a slight _____ effect.

9.  *Show how a marketing mix might be developed for marketing the services of a banker or a lawyer.*

A.  Service marketers have begun to think of attracting and pleasing customers and of _____ their services.

B.  Physicians and beauticians provide personal services, while bankers usually provide more _____ services.

TEST YOURSELF (Multiple Choice)

Test yourself by selecting the best answer.  Check your answers with
those at the end of this chapter.

1.  All nonpersonal promotional activity for which a fee is paid is
    called:

    A.  sales promotion
    B.  advertising
    C.  personal selling
    D.  sales promotion

2.  When a group of firms advertise a general class of products without
    mentioning brands, this is called:

    A.  primary demand advertising
    B.  selective demand advertising
    C.  pioneering advertising
    D.  generic advertising

3.  In advertising, AIDA stands for:

    A.  advertisement, increase, decisions, attraction
    B.  activity, intelligence, determination, allegiance
    C.  attention, interest, desire, action
    D.  ability, interest, desirability, attractiveness

4.  _____ is a situation in which there is one large buyer in the
    market.

    A.  Monopoly
    B.  Oligopoly
    C.  Monopolistic competition
    D.  Monopsony

5.  When a firm uses a low price when introducing a new product it is
    called:

    A.  skimming pricing
    B.  price lining
    C.  market penetration pricing
    D.  functional discount pricing

6.  A discount granted a buyer because of a difference in position in
    the distribution channel is called:

    A.  a functional discount
    B.  a trade position discount
    C.  a volume discount
    D.  a quantity discount

7.  A technique from economic theory which helps to estimate the "best" price and quantity produced in terms of greatest profit is called:

    A.  marginal analysis
    B.  price analysis
    C.  market analysis
    D.  demand analysis

8.  The most important media are (in order of importance):

    A.  television, newspapers, direct mail magazines
    B.  direct mail, television, newspapers, magazines
    C.  newspapers, television, direct mail, magazines
    D.  magazines, newspapers, direct mail, television

9.  Any of a variety of devices to increase sales, including trading stamps, contests, and special attractions is called:

    A.  personal selling
    B.  publicity
    C.  advertising
    D.  sales promotion

10. Customary price is important in understanding:

    A.  cost-plus pricing
    B.  demand-oriented pricing
    C.  trade-off pricing
    D.  skimming pricing


TEST YOURSELF (Ture-False)

Test yourself by answering whether the following statments are true or false.  Check your answers with those at the end of this chapter.

____  1.  When a group of firms advertise a general class of product without mentioning brands, this is called primary demand advertising.

____  2.  Advertising includes all personal promotional activity for which a fee is paid.

____  3.  The arrangement of parts in a print ad is called the layout.

____  4.  Prospecting is a very important part of the personal selling process.

____  5.  Public relations is communication through the news media as a legitimate part of the news.

___ 6. In a monopsony situation, there is one large buyer in the market.

___ 7. The cost approach to pricing is much more customer-oriented than the demand approach.

___ 8. A discount given to a channel member for performance of a specific marketing activity is called a functional discount.

___ 9. When a few firms sell highly similar products and dominate a market, this is called monopolistic competition.

___ 10. A low inventory turnover rate indicates efficiency in the use of resources.

EXERCISE 11-1

(To improve your understanding of personal selling, sales promotion, and publicity)

1. How does personal selling differ from advertising?



2. Although salespeople operate differently, most of them follow some sequence of activities.  What are those activities?



3. What are the major responsibilities of the sales manager?



4. Define the following terms and give examples of each:

   a.  sales promotion

   b.  publicity

   c.  point-of-purchase displays

5. "The effect of public relations on sales is usually indirect and long-run."  Explain this statement.

EXERCISE 11-2

(To review pricing approaches in retailing)

Ashker's Village Shoppe follows the cost-based pricing policy of marking up all clothing 75 percent on the store's unit cost.

1.  Find the markup and the selling price for the two items below:

|  | | Markup | Selling Price |
|---|---|---|---|
| #505 Pants suit | $18 | $_____ | $_____ |
| #X487 Cocktail dress | $64 | $_____ | $_____ |

2.  Recently the store has begun to experience a decline in its sales volume.  The manager believes that some sales are being lost to a new competitor in a nearby shopping center.  What other approach(es) to pricing might the firm consider adopting?  Discuss.

EXERCISE 11-3

(To improve your understanding of important pricing concepts)

1.  List and define the two major approaches to pricing new products.

    a.


    b.


2.  Discuss the two major approaches to setting the basic price of a product.

    a.


    b.


3.  Describe the following types of discounts:

    a.  cash discount


    b.  trade position discount


    c.  functional discount


    d.  quantity discount

EXERCISE 11-4

(Crossword Puzzle Review)

Across

3. Paid nonpersonal promotion
4. Radio, television, or print--
to advertising
6. Discount given to a marketing
channel member for a service
performed
7. You can buy beer this way or
by the sixpack; by the _____
9. What a price which is set high
on introduction of a new
product is designed to do to
the market
10. Country in North America (abbr)
13. What a price which is set low
on the introduction of a new
product is designed to do to
the market
14. Addition to cost by a middleman

Down

1. Consumption in a visible
way
2. For marketing, gathering,
recording, and analyzing
data
3. A firm which produces and
places ads for other firms
is an ad _____
5. Sales divided by average
inventory gives this rate
8. Creating a special marketing mix aimed at certain
potential buyers
11. Attention, interest, desire,
action--the _____
process
12. Research using original
information

16. Type of selling involving
    face-to-face contact
17. Competition with differen-
    tiated products is said to
    be this

15. In marketing, monetary cost
    and terms of sale

EXERCISE 11-5

(Incident: Diet Coke)

Answer the questions on a plain piece of paper.


For the first time in its history, the Coca-Cola Company in 1982 used the Coke trademark on a product other than Coke--diet Coke. Although the company makes other brands of soft drinks, none had previously been associated with Coke.

The decision to market diet Coke was a complex one.  Top management was especially concerned about the potential impact of diet Coke on "the real thing".  A total promotion budget of $100 million was established to back the new entry in the soft drink industry during the first two years of its life.  Half the budget was for advertising and the other half was for sales promotion.

Questions

1.  Why do you think top management was hesitant to use the Coke trademark on other products it marketed?

2.  What are the basic differences in promotional objectives for Coke and diet Coke?

3.  How would you recommend spending the funds budgeted for sales promotion?  Explain.

CHAPTER 11 ANSWERS

Test Your Business
Vocabulary

1. H (p. 312)      10. L (pp. 325-326)
2. M (p. 316)      11. Q (pp. 328-329)
3. P (p. 314)      12. V (p. 329)
4. A (pp. 317-318) 13. U (p. 330)
5. N (p. 319)      14. T (p. 330)
6. E (p. 323)      15. C (p. 329)
7. G (p. 324)      16. D (p. 327)
8. F (p. 325)      17. S (p. 323)
9. R (p. 325)      18. I (p. 331)

Programmed Review
(refer to the indicated pages
in the text)

1.                 6.
   A. (p. 312)        A. (p. 325)
   B. (p. 312)        B. (p. 327)
2.                 7.
   A. (p. 316)        A. (p. 329)
   B. (p. 316)        B. (p. 330)
3.                 8.
   A. (p. 318)        A. (p. 331)
   B. (p. 318)        B. (p. 331)
4.                 9.
   A. (p. 319)        A. (pp. 332-333)
   B. (p. 321)        B. (p. 332)
5.
   A. (p. 323)
   B. (p. 323)
   C. (p. 324)

Test Yourself (Multiple Choice)

1. B (p. 314)    6. B (p. 329)
2. A (p. 315)    7. A (p. 327)
3. C (pp. 317-318) 8. C (p. 315)
4. D (p. 325)    9. D (p. 324)
5. C (p. 329)   10. B (p. 327)

Test Yourself (True-False)

1. True (p. 315)   6. True (p. 325)
2. False (p. 314)  7. False (pp. 325-326)
3. True (p. 318)   8. True (p. 329)
4. True (p. 321)   9. False (p. 325)
5. False (p. 323) 10. False (p. 330)

Exercise 11-3

1a. market penetration
                (p. 329)
1b. market skimming
                (p. 330)
2a. cost approach
                (pp. 325-326)
2b. demand approach
                (p. 327)
3a-3d.  (pp. 328-329)

Exercise 11-4

Across:
3. advertising (p. 314)
4. media (p. 314)
6. functional (p. 329)
7. case
9. skim (p. 330)
10. USA
13. penetrate (p. 329)
14. markup (pp. 325-326)
16. personal (p. 319)
17. monopolistic (p. 325)

Down:
1. conspicuous
2. research
3. agency (p. 316)
5. turnover (p. 330)
8. segmentation
11. AIDA (pp. 317-318)
12. primary
13. price (p. 324)

# CHAPTER 12

# Accounting

Chapter 12 provides an introduction to accounting fundamentals. Accounting plays a very significant role in the functioning of any firm. It is the process of recording, gathering, manipulating, auditing, and interpreting information that describes the assets and operation of a firm. It aids in decision making.

Two broad categories of accounting, financial and managerial, are discussed and examples are presented. Financial accounting is designed to "keep tabs" on what a firm owns and to protect the property rights of the firm's owner(s). Managerial accounting provides information for a manager's own use in decision making. Both types of accounting provide important data for management in its attempt to achieve the firm's goals.

The two basic financial statements generated by accounting are the balance sheet and the income statement. The former presents a financial picture of a firm at one point in time. The income statement shows what actually happened over a period of time to explain some of the differences between successive balance sheets. Information from both statements allows prospective investors to evaluate and assess the organization's financial operations.

Accounting data can serve as the basis for both planning and controlling. The importance of this is seen in the use of financial ratios. A firm's financial condition, in terms of solvency, efficiency, and profitability can be determined from these ratios.

The final section elaborates on accounting's role in the budgeting process. A budget requires managers to plan carefully for the future and to critically examine present and past performance.

TEST YOUR BUSINESS VOCABULARY

Test your business vocabulary by matching each key concept with the proper phrase. Check your answers with those at the end of this chapter.

Key Concepts

___ 1. financial accounting
___ 2. managerial accounting
___ 3. assets
___ 4. equity
___ 5. liability
___ 6. revenue
___ 7. expense
___ 8. depreciation
___ 9. key ratio

___ 10. current ratio
___ 11. budget
___ 12. sales forecast
___ 13. responsibility accounting
___ 14. product cost accounting
___ 15. balance sheet
___ 16. net profit
___ 17. Certified Public Accountant
                   (CPA)
___ 18. income statement

Phrases

A. A register of financial value
B. Current assets divided by current liabilities
C. A statement of financial position
D. The using up of resources such as Supplies Used
E. A method of classifying cost information and thereby evaluating the performance of the components of the firm and their managers
F. What remains after expenses are deducted from revenues
G. Sales minus cost of goods sold
H. The claim of owners against resources of the firm
I. Claims on resources or assets
J. The accounting process directed toward the flow of resources, communicating with people outside the firm
K. Any financially significant event
L. A financial statement showing revenues, expenses, and profits of a firm during a given period of time
M. A financial ratio computed from items on the financial statements of a firm and used to evaluate the credit risk or financial strength of a firm
N. The accounting process internally directed to facilitate the firm's management
O. An accountant who has fulfilled legal requirements of his/her state for knowledge in accounting theory, practice, auditing, and law
P. Cash or property that can be quickly converted to cash
Q. A financial forecast showing expected income and expenditures for a given period of time
R. A deduction in the balance sheet to indicate a decline in value of a fixed asset over time
S. A firm's resources such as land, cash, and accounts receivable
T. The claim of a nonowner against a firm
U. Systems for allocating costs to products produced by a firm

V. An estimate of the sales that will be made in a future period of time
W. Inward flow of value to a firm
X. A conservative measure of owner's equity that excludes goodwill from assets

PROGRAMMED REVIEW

(To help you in understanding the chapter material and to see if you have mastered the objectives stated at the beginning of the chapter)

1. *Distinguish between financial and managerial accounting processes.*

    A. _____ accounting helps the manager to "keep score" for the firm.

    B. _____ accounting aids in planning and decision making.

2. *Identify the three principal tasks of accounting.*

    A. Accounting is designed to do its various jobs, such as_____

    _____, _____, and _____.

    B. The accounting system must provide clear and efficient estimates of _____ facts.

3. *Describe what a CPA does.*

    A. CPAs have fulfilled the _____ requirements of their states for knowledge in accounting.

    B. Much of the independent CPA's work is classified as _____, which involves checking the accuracy of records.

4. *Prepare a chart showing the major information flows of accounting.*

    A. Accounting traces a _____ of information flows.

    B. Accounting can be used to "account to" managers, _____,

    _____, and government.

5. *Explain the relationship between transactions and accounts.*

    A. A register of financial value is known as a(n) _____.

    B. A _____ is used to describe any change in an asset or an equity.

6. *Complete both of the principal accounting equations.*

   A.  Assets = _____ + Owner's Equity

   B.  _____ - Expenses = Net Profit

7. *Draw up a simple example of the two principal financial statements.*

   A.  A _____ _____ presents a financial picture of a firm at one point in time.

   B.  The _____ _____ summarizes the revenue and expense accounts.

8. *Explain the purpose of the two principal financial statements.*

   A.  The _____ _____ summarizes the asset and equity accounts.

   B.  Net sales, gross profit, and wages and salaries paid are examples of items found on the _____ _____.

9. *Demonstrate how an investor might use the statements of a firm he or she may wish to invest in.*

   A.  If you are interested in investing in the ABC Corporation, you will find information about net sales and expenses on the _____ _____.

10. *Explain and use at least one of the "key" ratios.*

    A.  The current ratio is computed by dividing _____ _____ by _____ _____.

    B.  Solvency, or _____ measurements are significant in evaluating a company's ability to meet short- and long-term obligations.

11. *Illustrate the managerial accounting concepts of budgeting and cost accounting.*

    A.  A budget is a formal dollar-and-cents statement of expected _____.

    B.  _____ accounting involves setting up responsibility centers in a firm.

    C.  _____ _____ accounting systems use cost centers to allocate all costs to the various products made by a firm.

TEST YOURSELF (Multiple Choice)

Test yourself by selecting the best answer.  Check your answers with
those at the end of this chapter.

1.  Financial accounting:

    A.  calls attention to business problems and the need for action
    B.  aids in planning and decision making
    C.  is aimed at control rather than valuation
    D.  watches the flow of resources and lets those who have an
        interest in them know where they stand

2.  Any change in an asset or an equity is called:

    A.  a transaction
    B.  a claim
    C.  a liability
    D.  an account

3.  Which of the following represents the basic accounting equation?

    A.  liabilities = assets + owner's equity
    B.  assets = liabilities + owner's equity
    C.  owner's equity + profit = assets
    D.  revenues + equity = assets

4.  The _____ _____ summarizes the asset and equity accounts.

    A.  income statement
    B.  profit-loss statement
    C.  balance sheet
    D.  equity statement

5.  The _____ _____ is a measure of liquidity.

    A.  current ratio
    B.  debt ratio
    C.  inventory ratio
    D.  accounting ratio

6.  A register of financial value is:

    A.  a statement
    B.  an entity
    C.  an account
    D.  a fiduciary

7.  A deduction in the balance sheet to indicate a decline in value of
    a fixed asset over time is called:

A.  devaluation
B.  equity
C.  value reassessment
D.  depreciation

8.  Asset accounts include:

A.  entities
B.  accounts receivable
C.  equities
D.  liabilities

9.  The difference between net sales and cost of goods sold is:

A.  gross profit
B.  a fixed asset
C.  a current liability
D.  owner's equity

10.  A formal dollar-and-cents statement of expected performance is:

A.  a system
B.  an accrual
C.  a budget
D.  a standard practice


TEST YOURSELF (True-False)

Test yourself by answering whether the following statements are true or false.  Check your answers with those at the end of this chapter.

____  1.  Accounting traces a sequence of information flows.
____  2.  The claims of outsiders are called a firm's expenses.
____  3.  Assets = liabilities is the most basic of all accounting equations.
____  4.  A balance sheet presents a financial picture of a firm at one point in time.
____  5.  A current asset is one that the firm normally expects to hold no longer than a year.
____  6.  Goodwill is the most tangible of all assets.
____  7.  The difference between net sales and cost of goods sold is gross profit.
____  8.  The sales forecast is the starting point for a general (master) budget.
____  9.  The simplest method of computing depreciation is the help-life method.
____ 10.  Key ratios are derived from financial statements.

EXERCISE 12-1

(To strengthen your understanding of accounting basics)

1. What is accounting?

2. Differentiate between managerial accounting and financial accounting.

3. List the four principal kinds of accounts.

    a.

    b.

    c.

    d.

4. List the three major classes of assets.

    a.

    b.

    c.

5. What does it mean to be a Certified Public Accountant (CPA)?

EXERCISE 12-2

(To help you understand financial ratios)

1.  What is the general purpose of financial ratios?

2.  List the three major categories of financial ratios.

    a.

    b.

    c.

3.  Define the following ratios (or show how they are calculated).

    a.  current ratio

    b.  sales-to-inventory ratio

EXERCISE 12-3

(To give you practice in solving accounting problems)

Show how you arrived at your answers.

1.  The Bowling Realty Company recently purchased a new typewriter.
    Its expected life is 10 years and Bowling uses the straight line
    depreciation method.  If the typewriter cost Bowling $500, how much
    would the first year's depreciation be?

2.  The Holston Stationery Shop showed the following items on its in-
    come statement:

    Net sales        $10,000
    Gross profit       6,000
    Wages paid         1,000

    The cost of goods sold is $_____.

3.  Given:  Beginning inventory        $ 40,000
            Purchases of merchandise     150,000
            Ending inventory              38,000

    Then the cost of goods sold is $_____.

4.  Given:  Stockholders' equity       $100,000
            Goodwill                      10,000

    Then tangible net worth is $_____.

5.  Given:  Current assets          $10,000
            Current liabilities       5,000
            Fixed assets              2,000

    Then the current ratio is_____.

6.  Given:  Net sales               $100,000
            Beginning inventory        50,000
            Ending inventory           30,000

    Then the sales-to-inventory ratio is_____.

EXERCISE 12-4

(Crossword Puzzle Review)

## Across

1. Occupation many business majors elect to pursue
4. Type of assets that have a life of more than one year
7. _____ _____ accounting allocates all costs to the various pro- ducts made by a firm
8. That which has been earned (mostly from sales)
10. Accounting term for the resources that are used up in performing the sales function (2 words)
12. To be speedy or rapid

## Down

1. Wages and salaries that are owed but not yet paid are said to _____
2. Last section that appears on a balance sheet (2 words)
3. A secretary must know how to do this
5. The financial statement that shows the profit or loss of a firm is a(n) _____ statement
6. Debts that must be paid in less than one year (2 words)
9. One of a firm's resources, like cash, land, buildings
11. Term for the work done by a CPA when checking the

14. Shows revenues, expenses, and profits; the income _____
16. Used by a baseball catcher
18. A preposition
19. Earnings from prior years that are plowed back into a firm
20. The opposite of huge
22. Type of accounting designed to communicate with people outside the firm
24. An owner's equity account for a proprietor or a partner
25. You should maintain a healthy one
26. Reward for the successful risk of one's investment in a business
27. The output of a data processing system relies on accurate _____
28. The income statement for Gloria's Dress Shop begins with _____ sales
29. A statement of financial position is also called a _____ sheet
30. Tangible net _____

accuracy of records
13. These are published by Dun and Bradstreet as an aid to financial analysis (2 words)
15. Financially significant event that must be recorded on the books of a firm
16. _____ accounting is internally directed to facilitate the firm's management
17. A Certified _____ Accountant
21. Term that describes the difference between actual and expected results
22. Although a popular craze, this is sometimes "here today and gone tomorrow"
23. A _____ based accounting system is often expensive but necessary

EXERCISE 12-5

(Incident: Depreciation and Disinflation)


Answer the questions on a plain piece of paper.


Depreciation is a non-cash, but tax-deductible, expense. It reduces the firm's tax liability. But because depreciation must be calculated on the basis of the historical cost of acquiring an asset, its value to a firm is effectively reduced during a period of high inflation. From the perspective of the depreciation allowance, therefore, high inflation rates tend to discourage firms from investing in new plants and equipment.

Beginning in 1982 our economy entered a period of disinflation. Disinflation means a sustained reduction in the inflation rate. It is not synonymous with deflation. Deflation means falling prices. Disinflation means that prices are rising, but at a declining rate.


Questions


1. On which financial statement does depreciation expense appear?


2. From the perspective of the depreciation allowance, why would high inflation rates tend to discourage firms from investing in new plants and equipment?


3. Refer to the "Authors' Commentary" on page 349 of the text. How would disinflation affect the relative attractiveness of valuing inventories according to the LIFO method?

Test Your Business
Vocabulary

| | |
|---|---|
| 1. J (p. 344) | 10. B (p. 359) |
| 2. N (p. 344) | 11. Q (p. 363) |
| 3. S (p. 348) | 12. V (p. 364) |
| 4. I (p. 348) | 13. E (p. 364) |
| 5. T (p. 348) | 14. U (p. 365) |
| 6. W (p. 349) | 15. C (p. 351) |
| 7. D (p. 349) | 16. F (p. 355) |
| 8. R (p. 353) | 17. O (p. 345) |
| 9. M (p. 358) | 18. L (P. 355) |

Programmed Review
(refer to the indicated pages in
the text)

| | |
|---|---|
| 1. | 7. |
| A. (p. 344) | A. (p. 351) |
| B. (P. 344) | B. (p. 355) |
| 2. | 8. |
| A. (p. 344) | A. (p. 355) |
| B. (p. 344) | B. (p. 354) |
| 3. | 9. |
| A. (p. 345) | A. (p. 354) |
| B. (p. 345 | |
| 4. | 10. |
| A. (p. 345) | A. (p. 359) |
| B. (pp. 345-347) | B. (p. 361) |
| 5. | 11. |
| A. (p. 348) | A. (p. 363) |
| B. (p. 350) | B. (p. 364) |
| 6. | C. (p. 365) |
| A. (p. 350) | |
| B. (p. 350) | |

Test Yourself (Multiple Choice)

| | |
|---|---|
| 1. D (p. 344) | 6. C (p. 348) |
| 2. A (p. 350) | 7. D (p. 353) |
| 3. B (p. 350) | 8. B (p. 352) |
| 4. C (p. 351) | 9. A (p. 355) |
| 5. A (p. 359) | 10. C (p. 363) |

Exercise 12-3

1. $500 divided by 10 = $50
   (p. 353)
2. $10,000 minus $6,000 = $4,000
   (pp. 354-355)
3. $40,000 plus $150,000 minus
   $38,000 = $152,000
   (pp. 354-355)
4. $100,000 minus $10,000 =
   $90,000   (pp. 353-354)
5. $10,000 divided by $5,000 = 2
   (p. 359)
6. $100,000 divided by the aver-
   age of $50,000 and $30,000
   ($40,000) = 2.5   (p. 359)

Exercise 12-4

1. (across) Accounting (p. 344)
1. (down) Accrue (p. 353)
2. Owners equity (p. 349)
3. Type
4. Fixed (p. 353)
5. Income (p. 355)
6. Current liabilities (p. 353)
7. Product cost (p. 365)
8. Revenue (p. 349)
9. Asset (p. 348)
10. Selling expenses
11. Auditing (p. 345)
12. Quick
13. Key ratios (p. 358)
14. Statement (p. 355)
15. Transaction (p. 350)
16. (across) Mitt
16. (down) Managerial (p. 344)
17. Public (p. 345)
18. At
19. Retained (p. 354)
20. Tiny
21. Variance
22. (across) Financial
22. (down) Fad
23. Computer (p. 365)
24. Capital (p. 354)
25. Diet
26. Profits (p. 350)
27. Input

Test Yourself (True-False)

1. True (p. 345)   6. False (p. 353)
2. False (p. 349)  7. True (p. 355)
3. False (p. 350)  8. True (p. 364)
4. True (p. 351)   9. False (p. 353)
5. True (p. 352)  10. True (p. 358)

28. Net (p. 354)
29. Balance (p. 351)
30  Worth

# CHAPTER 13

# Computers and Basic Quantitative Tools

Chapter 13 provides an introduction to the important concepts related to computers and quantitative methods. Computers are now commonplace and they impact on many phases of our daily lives. Computers help managers to make decisions and they also solve problems at home and provide entertainment. Computers are capable of storing and retrieving large amounts of data and performing mathematical calculations quickly.

Computer hardware and software are very important components of the system. The hardware consists of the machinery and electronic components. The tasks performed are input, storage, and output. The software complements hardware by giving instructions and setting hardware into motion. Software components may include time sharing, online real-time systems, and the languages.

The last portion of this chapter focuses on quantitative tools for management decisions. Statistics is discussed first. It provides a way of summarizing and interpreting numerical data. One method of data summarization is the computation of averages. The basic types of averages are the mean, mode, and median. Other tools discussed include sampling, breakeven analysis, and linear programming.

# TEST YOUR BUSINESS VOCABULARY

Test your business vocabulary by matching each key concept with the proper phrase. Check your answers with those at the end of this chapter.

## Key Concepts

___ 1. data processing
___ 2. word processing system
___ 3. software
___ 4. hardware
___ 5. online real-time system
___ 6. FORTRAN
___ 7. COBOL
___ 8. arithmetic mean
___ 9. median

___ 10. mode
___ 11. sample
___ 12. breakeven analysis
___ 13. statistics
___ 14. central processing unit (CPU)
___ 15. frequency distribution
___ 16. modem
___ 17. input-output (I-0) devices

## Phrases

A. it demonstrates the profitability of various levels of production
B. a specialized language that is extremely close to English and is used for business data processing
C. the accumulation, storage, sorting, interpretation, and reporting of facts in a numerical form
D. a kind of "average" computed by adding a group of values and dividing the total by the number of values
E. a science-oriented computer language
F. relatively new language which uses structured programming and is used in microcomputers
G. intervals or ranges of values are established first
H. a graphic representation of a frequency distribution
I. the most frequent value in an array
J. explanation or illustration of a computer program
K. it includes an internal memory, an arithmetic unit, a logic unit, and a control unit
L. any piece of equipment that allows information to be fed into a computer or permits the computer to make information available to its user
M. a device that converts direct current (DC) signals to tones and then converts them back to DC signals
N. numerical data
O. a part of a larger group that represents the larger group
P. the electronic and mechanical components of a data processing system
Q. the middle value of a group of values ranked in order of magnitude
R. a text-editing computer
S. the programs, languages, and routines used in electronic data processing
T. a computer system that permits direct and continuous access to stored information

U. explanation or illustration of a computer program

## PROGRAMMED REVIEW

(To help you in understanding the chapter material and to see if you have mastered the objectives stated at the beginning of the chapter)

1. *Describe one important way that a computer enters your life.*

   A. Small, special-purpose computers called _____ are being built into cars and appliances to improve their performance.

   B. A computer can store a huge mass of _____ and make thousands of routine calculations.

2. *Give some examples of common business applications of computers.*

   A. In the personnel administration area, the computer assists in preparing the monthly _____.

   B. Computers help in keeping track of _____ so firms will not run out of merchandise.

3. *Distinguish between automation, data processing, and word processing.*

   A. All businesses need to collect, store, manipulate, interpret, and report data. This is called _____ _____.

   B. A word-processing system is a _____-_____ computer.

4. *Draw a diagram of a computer system.*

   A. The heart of any computer is its _____ _____ _____.

   B. The tasks of inputting, storing, manipulating, and outputting are performed by four kinds of components. They are _____ devices, central processing units, outside data _____ systems, and _____ devices.

5. *Recognize common input-output devices for computers.*

   A. Input and output devices are the _____ used in getting information in and out of the computer.

   B. As a group, input and output devices, which are pieces of hardware, are known as _____ equipment.

6. *Explain the function of software.*

A. Computer _____ complements hardware by giving instructions and setting hardware into motion.

B. When system software enables a computer to allow many users to interact with the computer at the same time, this is called _____ _____.

C. Systems software programs are written in _____ language.

D. _____ has become the most widely implemented langauge for microcomputers.

7. *Explain the impact of microcomputers on business.*

A. Small systems have been marketed with broad _____ packages and specialized programs tailored for many industries.

B. Microcomputers enhance large-scale computers by placing additional computing power throughout the organization. Such linkages are called _____.

8. *Contrast several ways that people react to computers.*

A. _____ reactions to the computer range from worship to outright fear.

B. Closely related to the question of privacy is the fear of loss through _____ crime.

9. *Compute an arithmetic mean and median.*

A. The _____ is the middle number when numbers are listed in a rank from smallest to largest.

B. The arithmetic mean is an _____ computed by first adding numbers, finding the total, and then dividing that total by the number of numbers that were added together.

10. *Prepare a breakeven chart.*

A. Breakeven analysis demonstrates the profitability of various levels of _____.

B. The two kinds of costs are _____ and _____.

TEST YOURSELF (Multiple Choice)

Test yourself by selecting the best answer. Check your answers with those at the end of this chapter.

1. A detailed set of instructions in a special computer language is called:

   A. a computer program
   B. computer hardware
   C. the central processing unit
   D. internal memory

2. Which of the following tasks is not performed by computer hardware?

   A. input
   B. storage and/or manipulation
   C. output
   D. data interpretation

3. The most frequent value in an array is called:

   A. the mean
   B. the mode
   C. the median
   D. the geometric mean

4. A science-oriented computer language is called:

   A. BASIC
   B. COBOL
   C. FORTRAN
   D. Pascal

5. The accumulation, storage, manipulation, interpretation, and reporting of data are called:

   A. linear programming
   B. data processing
   C. automation
   D. computer programming

6. Which of the following are items of computer software?

   A. computer programs
   B. input devices
   C. outside memories
   D. central processing units

7. Methods of using mathematics and statistics to help solve business problems and understand facts is called:

   A. qualitative tools
   B. behavioral tools
   C. analytical tools
   D. quantitative tools

8. The _____ _____ shows at which level total costs are exactly equal to total sales revenue.

   A. breaking point
   B. equilibrium point
   C. breakeven point
   D. profitability point

9. The _____ includes an internal memory, an arithmetic unit, a logic unit, and a control unit.

   A. central processing unit
   B. computer program
   C. input-output device
   D. online system

10. Which of the following costs is most dependent on the number of units produced and sold?

   A. fixed cost
   B. permanent cost
   C. flexible cost
   D. variable cost


TEST YOURSELF (True-False)

Test yourself by answering whether the following statements are true or false. Check your answers with those at the end of this chapter.

____ 1. Businesses use computers to control production costs.

____ 2. The size of the data flow and the financial resources of the organization determine the scale and complexity of its data processing system.

____ 3. The software consists of the machinery and electronic components.

____ 4. Batch processing is data processing in which data are collected for a period of time before being entered into the computer system.

____ 5. The ages of employees in the data processing department of Ashker, Inc. are 28, 30, 26, 35, 38, 22, 24, 29, and 39. The mean age is 25.

____ 6. Overhead costs are the same as variable costs.

____ 7. The heart of any computer is its central processing unit.

___ 8. Controllers regulate the "traffic" of peripheral hardware into the CPU.

___ 9. COBOL stands for Common Basic Oriented Language.

___ 10. Statistical sampling is a frequently used quantitative tool.

EXERCISE 13-1

(To help you review the basics of computers)

1.  List seven applications of computers in business firms.

    a.

    b.

    c.

    d.

    e.

    f.

    g.

2.  List the three tasks that are performed by computer hardware.

    a.

    b.

    c.

3.  List the four kinds of parts, or components, that perform the three tasks you listed in 2 above.

    a.

    b.

    c.

    d.

4.  List the three most commonly used computer languages.

    a.

    b.

    c.

EXERCISE 13-2

(To improve your understanding of some quantitative tools for management decisions)

1.  Given the following set of numbers

        4

        8

        14

        20

        25

        25

        30

    a.  What is the median?

    b.  What is the mode?

    c.  What is the arithmetic mean?

2.  Prepare a frequency distribution of the following exam scores:

    | 10 | 40 | 65 | 70 | 98 | 92 |
    |----|----|----|----|----|----|
    | 45 | 50 | 99 | 50 | 88 | 45 |
    | 50 | 75 | 98 | 60 | 82 | 70 |
    | 30 | 95 | 88 | 84 | 98 | 78 |
    | 90 | 100| 97 | 75 | 99 | 68 |
    | 80 | 85 | 86 | 99 | 89 | 71 |
    | 60 | 40 | 80 | 76 | 91 | 72 |

    Arrange the distribution by letter grade as follows:

    A = 90-100

    B = 80-89.9

    C = 70-79.9

    D = 60-69.9

    F =  0-59.9

3.  On a plain piece of paper, prepare a histogram of the data in 2 above.

4. Answer the following questions pertaining to breakeven analysis.

   a. Define breakeven analysis

   b. Give examples of fixed costs and variable costs as they relate
      to breakeven analysis

   c. Given the following information, compute the breakeven point.
      Al's Toy Manufacturing Co has total fixed costs of $50,000,
      unit variable cost of $3.50, and unit price of $10.50.  What is
      the breakeven point?

EXERCISE 13-3

(To improve your understanding of the selection and installation of
computers and how people react to computers)

1. What are some of the basic questions asked during the following
   phases of computer evaluation?

   a. hardware evaluation phase




   b. software evaluation phase




   c. vendor evaluation phase




2. Computers are an integral part of our way of life.  Discuss some
   of the human reactions to computers.

EXERCISE 13-4

(Word Puzzle)

Arranged in a column below is one of the key concepts from this chapter. Opposite each letter of this concept is the definition of another key concept also found in this chapter. Fill in the blanks provided with the remaining letters of the defined key concept.

C _ _ _ _                    1. Common Business Oriented Language.

_ O _ _ _                    2. A device used to connect typewriter terminals to the CPU by means of telephone lines.

_ _ M _ _ _                  3. A part of a larger group.

_ P _ _ _ _ _ _ _

                             4. Techniques used to solve problems of scheduling; _____ research.

_ _ _ U _ _ _ _ _ _ _        5. An explanation of what a program does, how it is used, and how it works.

_ _ _ T _ _ _ _              6. It gives instructions and sets hardware into motion.

_ _ _ E                      7. The most frequent number in a list.

_ _ _ _ _ _ _ R _ _ _        8. It permits many users of a computer to interact at the same time.

EXERCISE 13-5

(Incident: Humanizing Computers)

Answer the questions on a plain piece of paper.

Computer manufacturers are turning more and more to emphasizing human factors in the design of their hardware and software. Human factors engineering, or ergonomics, has become very important.

The goal is to make computers that are more suitable to humans. This includes making computers that complement human capabilities instead of overwhelming them. For example, computers must be easy to operate and comfortable to use. It also includes making the command system in the program such that the user can follow the machine's logic without feeling threatened or frustrated.

Questions

1. Do you think that improvements in human factors engineering are partly responsible for the big boom in sales of "home" micro-computers? Explain.

2. Why do some people fear computers? Can greater attention by computer manufacturers to human factors engineering help people who fear computers to overcome their fear? Explain.

3. Give an example of how computers and people can complement each other.

Test Your Business Vocabulary

| | |
|---|---|
| 1. C (p. 375) | 10. I (p. 393) |
| 2. R (p. 375) | 11. O (pp. 394-395) |
| 3. S (p. 382) | 12. A (p. 395) |
| 4. P (p. 376) | 13. N (p. 392) |
| 5. T (p. 383) | 14. K (p. 377) |
| 6. E (p. 384) | 15. G (p. 393) |
| 7. B (p. 384) | 16. M (p. 380) |
| 8. D (p. 392) | 17. L (p. 378) |
| 9. Q (p. 392) | |

Programmed Review
(refer to the indicated pages
in the text)

1.
  A. (p. 370)
  B. (p. 371)
2.
  A. (p. 371)
  B. (p. 371)
3.
  A. (p. 375)
  B. (p. 375)
4.
  A. (p. 377)
  B. (p. 377)
5.
  A. (p. 378)
  B. (p. 378)

6.
  A. (p. 382)
  B. (p. 383)
  C. (p. 383)
  D. (p. 384)
7.
  A. (p. 382)
  B. (p. 382)
8.
  A. (p. 389)
  B. (p. 389)
9.
  A. (p. 392)
  B. (p. 392)
10.
  A. (p. 395)
  B. (p. 395)

Exercise 13-1

1. (p. 372)
2. (p. 376)
3. (p. 377)
4. (p. 384)

Exercise 13-4

1. COBOL (p. 384)
2. modem (p. 380)
3. sample (p. 394)
4. operations (p. 397)
5. documentation (p. 385)
6. software (p. 382)
7. mode (p. 393)
8. time sharing (p. 383)

Test Yourself (Multiple Choice)

| | |
|---|---|
| 1. A (p. 376) | 6. A (pp.382-383) |
| 2. D (p. 376) | 7. D (p. 392) |
| 3. B (p. 393) | 8. C (p. 395) |
| 4. C (p. 384) | 9. A (p. 377) |
| 5. B (p. 375) | 10. D (p. 396) |

Test Yourself (True-False)

| | |
|---|---|
| 1. True (p. 372) | 6. False (p. 395) |
| 2. True (p. 375) | 7. True (p. 377) |
| 3. False (p. 382) | 8. True (p. 383) |
| 4. True (p. 383) | 9. False (p. 384) |
| 5. False (pp. 392-393) | 10. True (pp. 394-395) |

# CHAPTER 14

# Banks and Other
# Financial Institutions

Financial institutions play a pivotal role in our economic system. This chapter describes some of the functions of these diverse institutions. The institutions discussed are as follows: commercial banks, savings and loan associations, trust companies, credit unions, life insurance companies, factoring companies, commercial finance companies, sales finance companies, consumer finance companies, and commercial paper houses. All of these institutions have their respective roles and functions to perform. They also provide financial alternatives for individuals and businesses.

In addition to discussing financial institutions, the structure and purpose of the Federal Reserve System is presented. The Federal Reserve is the central bank of the United States. Its main purpose is to control the nation's money supply. In order to perform this function the Fed uses the tools of reserve requirement, margin requirement, and interest ceilings.

# TEST YOUR BUSINESS VOCABULARY

Test your business vocabulary by matching each key concept with the proper phrase. Check your answers with those at the end of this chapter.

## Key Concepts

___ 1. commercial bank
___ 2. Federal Deposit Insurance
       Corporation (FDIC)
___ 3. trust company
___ 4. credit union
___ 5. sales finance company
___ 6. demand deposit

___ 7. time deposit
___ 8. reserve requirement
___ 9. margin requirement
___ 10. savings bank
___ 11. commercial paper house
___ 12. Federal Reserve System
___ 13. prime rate of interest

## Phrases

A. a cooperative savings association that is owned by its depositors who work for the same employer or are members of the same nonbusiness organization
B. a mutual or stock company that shares risk with its policyholders for payment of a premium
C. a company that buys commercial paper directly from issuing corporations and resells it to buyers
D. a company that buys accounts receivable from a firm
E. major services are accepting demand deposits and making short-term loans
F. a bank that serves small savers by accepting their deposits and paying them interest on their savings
G. the percentage that buyers of securities must put up in cash when they buy them
H. anything that people will generally accept in payment of debts
I. the percentage of deposits that member banks of the Federal Reserve System must keep in vault cash or as deposits with their Federal Reserve Banks
J. fund that invests in commercial paper, bank certificates of deposit, and United States securities with high interest yields
K. this agency was created to insure national banks' depositors
L. checking accounts
M. it was created by the Federal Reserve Act of 1913
N. this amount is charged to best customers of large commercial banks
O. savings accounts and certificates of deposit are examples
P. a company that safeguards funds and estates entrusted to it
Q. a firm that specializes in financing installment purchases made by individuals and firms
R. it permits payment of interest on a checking account as long as a minimum balance is kept

PROGRAMMED REVIEW

(To help you in understanding the chapter material and to see if you
have mastered the objectives stated at the beginning of the chapter)

1. *Describe the commercial bank and its services.*

    A.  A commercial bank is a privately-owned, _____-seeking firm
        that serves individuals, nonbusiness organizations, and

        _____.

    B.  Commercial banks are the main source of _____-_____
        loans for business firms.

2. *Explain the functions of the FDIC.*

    A.  All national banks must carry _____ insurance and most
        state banks voluntarily do so.

    B.  Each insured bank pays a fee, based on its _____ _____,
        for this insurance.

    C.  Congress created the FDIC in _____.

3. *Discuss the future of electronic funds transfer.*

    A.  _____transfers let you pay for retail pur-
        chases with your EFT card.

    B.  _____systems permit you to telephone your
        financial institution and instruct it to pay certain bills.

4. *Compare and contrast the operations of savings banks, savings and
    loan associations, and credit unions.*

    A.  The two types of savings banks are _____ companies and
        _____ companies.

    B.  A _____ and _____ _____ accepts deposits from
        the general public and lends funds mainly for mortgages on
        homes and other real estate.

    C.  A _____ __ _____ is a cooperative savings association
        formed by the employees of a company.

5. *Outline the functions of commercial finance companies, sales
    finance companies, and factoring companies.*

    A.  A _____ _____ buys accounts receivable from a firm.

B.  A _____ _____ company specializes in financing installment purchases made by individuals and firms.

C.  A _____ _____ company makes loans to firms with accounts receivable, inventories, or equipment used as security for the loans.

6.  *Explain the roles of trust companies, consumer finance companies, and commercial paper houses.*

A.  A consumer finance company makes personal loans to _____.

B.  In many cases a commercial paper house acts as a _____ who charges a commission for bringing the issuing company and a buyer together.

C.  A _____ company safeguards property entrusted to it.

7.  *Explain the growth of money market mutual funds and "all-in-one" financial instituions in recent years.*

A.  Another name for the "all-in-one" institution is the _____ institution.

B.  At some point _____ forces might block the growth of "all-in-one" institutions for fear of monopolies in the money market.

8.  *Discuss the various forms of commercial bank deposits.*

A.  A _____ deposit is a checking account.

B.  A _____ deposit is one that is to remain with the bank for a period of time.

C.  The two types of time deposits are regular _____ accounts and _____ of deposit.

9.  *Describe the loan function of the commercial bank and the role of the prime rate.*

A.  The prime rate of interest is the _____ rate charged to major business customers by a specific large bank.

B.  Commercial banks offer both secured and _____ loans.

10. *Develop an example showing how the commercial banking system creates money.*

A.  Banks subject to federal regulation must keep some portion of their demand deposits in vault cash or as deposits with the Federal Reserve Bank. This amount is known as _____ _____.

B. The process of creating money is known as _____ expansion.

11. *Describe the structure of the Federal Reserve System.*

    A. The Federal Reserve System is the _____ bank of the United States.

    B. The board of governors of the Fed is composed of _____ members.

    C. The main purpose of the Fed is to control the nation's _____ _____.

12. *Outline the operations of the Fed.*

    A. The Federal Open Market Committee sets the Fed's open market policy by directing the Federal Reserve Banks either to _____ or _____ government securities.

    B. The _____ _____ is the percentage that buyers of corporate securities must pay in cash when they buy securities.

    C. The buying of government securities is designed to _____ business activity and increase the money supply.

TEST YOURSELF (Multiple Choice)

Test yourself by selecting the best answer. Check your answers with those at the end of this chapter.

1. The prime rate of interest is:

    A. the rate charged to the most risky borrowers
    B. the rate charged by banks on consumer installment notes
    C. the rate charged on time deposits
    D. the rate charged the least risky borrowers

2. A checking account at a commercial bank can also be called:

    A. a time deposit
    B. a demand deposit
    C. immediate withdrawal account
    D. money market account

3. A firm which buys accounts receivable from firms for less than their face value and collects them for its own account is:

    A. a sales finance company
    B. a credit union

C. a factoring company
D. a trust

4. A mutual or stock company that shares risk with its policyholders for payment of a premium is called:

A. a credit union
B. a life insurance company
C. a trust company
D. a commercial finance company

5. The percentage that buyers of securities must put up in cash when they buy them is called the:

A. margin requirement
B. reserve requirement
C. protection margin
D. security requirement

6. The Federal Reserve System is

A. a union of commercial banks
B. the central bank of the United States
C. a credit-granting institution but not a commercial bank
D. none of the above

7. Which of the following is not an activity of the Federal Reserve System?

A. controlling the money supply
B. setting interest ceilings
C. clearing checks
D. providing loans to household consumers

8. In an effort to stimulate the level of business activity the Federal Reserve System is likely to take which one of the following courses of action?

A. buy government securities
B. raise the discount rate
C. raise the reserve requirement
D. none of the above

9. The main source of short-term loans for business firms is:

A. savings banks
B. credit unions
C. commercial banks
D. money market mutual funds

10. The board of governors of the Federal Reserve System is composed
    of _____ members.

    A. 6
    B. 9
    C. 5
    D. 7

TEST YOURSELF (True-False)

Test yourself by answering whether the following statements are true or
false. Check your answers with those at the end of the chapter.

____ 1. The heart of our banking system is the commercial bank.

____ 2. Deregulation of banks and savings and loan associations has
        reduced competition with each other.

____ 3. A time deposit is a checking account on which interest is paid.

____ 4. The United States is divided into 12 Federal Reserve Bank dis-
        tricts.

____ 5. The reserve requirement is the percentage that buyers of cor-
        porate securities must pay in cash when they buy securities.

____ 6. The discount rate is the interest rate charged by Federal
        Reserve Banks to member banks that borrow money.

____ 7. One way for the Federal Reserve Board to slow down business
        activities is to sell government securities.

____ 8. General Motors Acceptance Corporation (GMAC) and General
        Electric Credit Corporation are examples of sales finance
        companies.

____ 9. Promissory notes are one of the least used credit instruments
        for getting short-term funds.

____10. The prime rate of interest is the lowest rate charged to major
        business customers by a specific large bank.

EXERCISE 14-1

(To strengthen your understanding of financial institutions)

1. Define or describe the following:

    a. commercial banks

    b. savings banks

    c. savings and loan associations

    d. trust companies

    e. credit unions

    f. factoring companies

    g. sales finance companies

    h. consumer finance companies

2. List some of the important services provided by commercial banks.

| | |
|---|---|
| a. | g. |
| b. | h. |
| c. | i. |
| d. | j. |
| e. | k. |
| f. | l. |

EXERCISE 14-2

(To help you understand the creation of money and the actions of the
Federal Reserve System in influencing business activity)

1.  You just broke open your piggybank and you deposited $500 in paper
    currency and coins in your checking account at First National Bank.
    All banks in this exercise are subject to a reserve requirement of
    15 percent.  Assume that no borrower takes part of his or her loan
    in cash and that the banks want to lend as much as they legally can.
    Complete the following.

| Bank | New Deposit | New Loan | Legal Reserve |
|------|-------------|----------|---------------|
| Your bank | $500.00 | $425.00 | $75.00 |
| Bank 2 | _____ | _____ | _____ |
| Bank 3 | _____ | _____ | _____ |
| Bank 4 | _____ | _____ | _____ |
| Bank 5 | _____ | _____ | _____ |
| Total for entire banking system | _____ | _____ | _____ |

2.  Write the number of the proper action under the appropriate headings.

    *To stimulate business activity:*      *To slow down business activity:*

    _____                                _____

    _____                                _____

    _____                                _____

    1.  Buy government securities
    2.  Sell government securities
    3.  Raise the discount rate
    4.  Lower the discount rate
    5.  Lower the reserve requirement
    6.  Raise the reserve requirement

EXERCISE 14-3

(To improve your understanding of selected aspects of Federal Reserve operations)

1.  Discuss the three ways that Federal Reserve System actions can be used to stimulate business activity.

    a.

    b.

    c.

2.  Discuss the three ways that Federal Reserve System actions can be used to slow down business activity.

    a.

    b.

    c.

3.  Using an example illustrate the various stages a check goes through to be cleared through the Federal Reserve System.

EXERCISE 14-4

(Scrambled Word Puzzle)

The letters for some of the key concepts from this chapter are scrambled on the left. Unscramble them and match each key concept with its definition somewhere in the right column.

1. ENYOM

2. TUNOICREDNI

3. YNAPMOCTSURT

4. DDDNAMEPESOTI

5. TTIIEMSOPED

6. EEEEEESRRVRQIRUTNM

7. TENMERIUQERNIGRAM

8. NAKBSGINVAS

9. PMOCNYAGFINRTOCA

10. EVRESERMETSYSDEFREAL

A. It buys accounts receivable from firms.

B. A cooperative savings association formed by the employees of a company.

C. It safeguards property entrusted to it.

D. The Fed.

E. Paper currency, coins, checkable deposits at banks and other financial institutions.

F. It serves small savers by accepting their deposits and paying them interest on their savings.

G. A checking account.

H. Interest is paid to depositors during the time their money is on deposit in the bank.

I. The percentage of their deposits that member banks have to keep in vault cash or as deposits with their FRBs.

J. The percentage that buyers of corporate securities must pay in cash when they buy securities.

EXERCISE 14-5

(Incident:  The Fed Lowers the Discount Rate)


Answer the questions on a plain piece of paper.


One of the Federal Reserve System's major activities is control-ling the nation's money supply.  In the summer of 1982, the Fed apparently believed that it had the growth in the nation's money supply under control and it could ease up on credit.  Thus in July 1982 the Fed reduced its discount rate from 12 percent to 11.5 percent.  The following month the Fed reduced its discount rate again--from 11.5 percent to 11 percent.  This brought the discount rate to its lowest level since late 1980.

The Fed hoped that its actions would help to push interest rates down.  Among other things, high interest rates were being blamed for the recession and a large and growing number of corporate bankruptcies.  Almost immediately after the reductions in the discount rate, short-term interest rates started declining and major banks were lowering their prime interest rate.


Questions

1.  What is the discount rate?

2.  Would the Fed's lowering of the discount rate tend to stimulate or slow down business activity?  Explain.

3.  What is the prime rate of interest?

4.  Why would major banks tend to lower their prime rate of interest when the Fed lowers its discount rate?

# CHAPTER 14 ANSWERS

## Test Your Business Vocabulary

1. E (p. 411)
2. K (p. 412)
3. P (p. 416)
4. A (p. 417)
5. Q (p. 418)
6. L (p. 423)
7. O (p. 423)
8. I (p. 431)
9. G (p. 431)
10. F (p. 414)
11. C (p. 419)
12. M (p. 427)
13. N (p. 426)

## Programmed Review
(refer to the indicated pages in the text)

1.
   A. (p. 411)
   B. (p. 411)
2.
   A. (p. 412)
   B. (p. 412)
   C. (p. 412)
3.
   A. (pp. 412-413
   B. (p. 412)
4.
   A. (p. 414)
   B. (p. 414)
   C. (p. 414)
5.
   A. (p. 417)
   B. (p. 418)
   C. (p. 418)
6.
   A. (p. 418)
   B. (p. 419)
   C. (p. 416)

7.
   A. (p. 419)
   B. (p. 423)
8.
   A. (p. 423)
   B. (p. 423)
   C. (p. 423)
9.
   A. (p. 426)
   B. (p. 426)
10.
   A. (p. 426)
   B. (p. 426)
11.
   A. (p. 427)
   B. (p. 427)
   C. (p. 427)
12.
   A. (p. 429)
   B. (p. 431)
   C. (p. 431)

## Test Yourself (True-False)

1. True (p. 411)
2. False (p. 413)
3. False (p. 423)
4. True (p. 428)
5. False (p. 431)
6. True (p. 430)
7. True (p. 431)
8. True (p. 418)
9. False (p. 419)
10. True (p. 426)

## Test Yourself (Multiple Choice)

1. D (p. 426)
2. B (p. 423)
3. C (p. 417)
4. B (p. 417)
5. A (p. 431)
6. B (p. 427)
7. D (pp. 430-431)
8. A (p. 431)
9. C (p. 411)
10. D (p. 427)

Exercise 14-2

| | New Deposit | New Loan | Legal Reserve |
|---|---|---|---|
| 1. Bank 2 | $ 425.00 | $ 361.25 | $ 63.75 |
| Bank 3 | 361.25 | 307.06 | 54.19 |
| Bank 4 | 307.06 | 261.00 | 46.06 |
| Bank 5 | 261.00 | 221.85 | 39.15 |
| Total for entire banking system | $3,333.33 | $2,833.33 | $ 500.00 |

Example on page 427.

2.  To stimulate business activity: 1,4,5  (p. 431)
    To slow down business activity: 2,3,6  (p. 431)


Exercise 14-4

1-E  money (p. 410)
2-B  credit union (p. 417)
3-C  trust company (p. 416)
4-G  demand deposit (p. 423)
5-H  time deposit (p. 423)
6-I  reserve requirement (p. 431)
7-J  margin requirement (p. 431)
8-F  savings bank (p. 414)
9-A  factoring company (p. 417)
10-D  Federal Reserve System (p. 427)

# Short-Term Financing and Risk Management

For business firms to continue their daily operations, some forms of financing and risk management must take place. This chapter outlines some of the diverse aspects of financial planning for the firm. Financial managers are responsible for evaluating and selecting from alternative sources of funds as well as managing risk. The two general sources of funds from which to choose are debt financing and equity financing.

Firms have two basic financial needs. These needs are for short-term, working capital and for intermediate and long-term capital. The three principal sources of short-term funds are trade credit, commercial bank loans, and commercial paper. Sources of long-term funds will be discussed in Chapter 16. It is the job of the financial manager to determine the most appropriate source of funds to meet the objectives of the firm.

Risk management is another aspect of sound financial planning. There are risks in everything and the degree of risk varies considerably. There are three approaches to dealing with risk. One is to assume risk yourself. The second is to avoid or reduce it. The third approach is to shift the risk to others. These approaches may be used together.

The final section focuses on types of insurance. The two types of insurance, from the perspective of the business firm, are property and casualty and life insurance. Each one has numerous forms and types from which to select. The type and amount of insurance should be consistent with the needs of the organization.

# TEST YOUR BUSINESS VOCABULARY

Test your business vocabulary by matching each key concept with the proper phrase. Check your answers with those at the end of this chapter.

Key Concepts

____ 1. working capital
____ 2. liquidity
____ 3. opportunity costs
____ 4. debt financing
____ 5. equity financing
____ 6. line of credit
____ 7. pure risk
____ 8. speculative risk

____ 9. promissory note
____ 10. trade credit
____ 11. law of large numbers
____ 12. principle of indemnity
____ 13. property and casualty
      insurance
____ 14. trade draft
____ 15. floor planning
____ 16. secured loans

Phrases

A. the use of borrowed funds
B. it includes those assets that flow regularly in the day-to-day operations of a firm--cash, accounts receivable, and inventories
C. open book account
D. the lender is protected by a pledge of the borrower's assets
E. a written promise by a customer to pay a certain sum of money to a supplier at a specified future date
F. an order to pay prepared by the supplier
G. assuming your own risk and preparing for loss
H. there is no chance of gain
I. mortality tables are based on this concept
J. there is the possibility of gains as well as losses
K. the ability to make payments that are due
L. losing the option of using funds in another way
M. funds provided by owners
N. commitment by a bank to lend up to a stated amount with minor restrictions
O. a special form of secured financing often used by automobile dealers
P. usually includes perils of fire, windstorm, flood, theft, loss of health, and liability due to negligence
Q. the insured cannot collect more than the actual cash value of the loss

## PROGRAMMED REVIEW

(To help you in understanding the chapter material and to see if you have mastered the objectives stated at the beginning of the chapter)

1. *Identify a financial manager's three principal duties.*

   A. The financial manager should manage _____ while maximizing the firm's return on assets.

   B. Another responsibility of the financial manager is to evaluate and select from alternative sources of _____.

2. *Outline the general sources of funds and the criteria for evaluating them.*

   A. _____ financing is the use of borrowed funds.

   B. _____ financing means the provision of funds by the owners.

   C. _____ is the factor of time of repayment.

3. *Draw a chart showing the normal flows of working capital in a manufacturing firm.*

   A. Working capital is a term applied to a firm's investment in

   _____-_____ assets.

   B. Current assets are those that flow regularly in the day-to-day operations of a firm, such as cash, _____ receivable, and

   _____.

   C. Cash and checking accounts are reduced by payments to _____ and payments of notes to banks.

4. *Illustrate the use of two major sources of short-term credit--trade credit and commercial bank loans.*

   A. Trade credit is credit extended by _____ to _____.

   B. _____ _____ is a very formal and specific agreement that guarantees funds for a period of time with strict rules limiting the borrower.

   C. When a _____ _____ _____ is set, the bank stands ready to lend up to this amount to the borrower with some restrictions.

5. *Distinguish between promissory notes and drafts.*

   A.  A promissory note is a _____ that is made
       by the maker, the person who promises to make the payment.

   B.  A draft is an _____ that is made by
       the drawer, the person who is to receive the payment.

6. *Explain the relationship between risk avoidance, self-insurance,
   and risk management.*

   A.  _____ - _____ means assuming your own risk and pre-
       paring for loss.

   B.  Risk the chance of _____.

7. *Distinguish between pure and speculative risk.*

   A.  _____ risks are those that offer only a chance of loss.

   B.  _____ risks are "gambles" in which there is possible gain
       as well as loss.

8. *Show how the law of large numbers is used to figure insurance
   premiums.*

   A.  _____ _____ are used to predict the number of policy-
       holders who will die in a given year.

   B.  If an insurance firm has a _____ number of policyholders,
       it can pretty well predict who many of them will die in a
       given year.

9. *Provide a brief explanation of the major types of insurance.*

   A.  _____ and _____ insurance traditionally includes
       perils of fire, windstorm, flood, theft, burglary, accident,
       loss of health, and liability due to negligence.

   B.  With life insurance, the insurer pays a _____ _____
       to a surviving person or firm upon the death of the person
       insured.

   C.  The major classes of life insurance policies are _____
       policies, _____ _____ policies, and _____

       _____ policies.

TEST YOURSELF (Multiple Choice)

Test yourself by selecting the best answer.  Check you answers with those at the end of this chapter.

1. Costs of losing the option to use the funds in another way are called:

   A. economic costs
   B. variable costs
   C. opportunity costs
   D. sunk costs

2. _____ tables are used to predict the number of policyholders who will die in a given year.

   A. Morality
   B. Mortality
   C. Morbidity
   D. Mortgage

3. _____ financing is the use of borrowed funds.

   A. Debt
   B. Leverage
   C. Liquidity
   D. Equity

4. A risk in which there is the possibility of gain as well as the possibility of loss is:

   A. a pure risk
   B. an adulterated risk
   C. a speculative risk
   D. planned risk

5. A loan which is secured is a loan in which:

   A. the lender is protected by a pledge of the borrower's assets
   B. a third party takes possession of the money, securing it from the borrower
   C. the interest rate is generally higher than if the note were not secured
   D. the lender is protected by the force of the borrower's good name

6. The ability to make payments that are due is the test of a firm's:

   A. working capital
   B. leverage
   C. short-term market value
   D. liquidity

7. Life insurance policies that are issued for definite time spans such as 5, 10, or 15 years are called:

    A. ordinary life policies
    B. term policies
    C. casualty policies
    D. extraordinary life policies

8. An order to pay that is made by the drawer is called:

    A. a promissory note
    B. a trade acceptance
    C. a draft
    D. a secured order

9. Which of the following is a current liability included in flows of working capital?

    A. accounts receivable
    B. finished goods inventory
    C. cash
    D. accounts payable

10. Which of the following is not one of the basic approaches to dealing with risk?

    A. self-insurance
    B. avoid or reduce risk
    C. depend on fate
    D. shift the risk to others

TEST YOURSELF (True-False)

Test yourself by answering whether the following statements are true or false. Check your answers with those at the end of this chapter.

____ 1. Equity and debt financing differ in the way they affect the claims on assets and earnings.

____ 2. Maturity is the factor of time of repayment.

____ 3. Economic costs are costs of losing the option to use the funds in another way.

____ 4. Floor planning is a special kind of secured financing.

____ 5. The principle of indemnity states that the insurance company must pay off the entire face value of the policy if total loss occurs.

____ 6. A time draft specifies a certain future date on which the draft must be paid.

___ 7. Insurance is available only for pure risks.

___ 8. Surety bonds do not protect the insured against loss from nonperformance of a contractual obligation.

___ 9. Trade credit is a major source of long-term funds.

___ 10. Most business property is underinsured.

EXERCISE 15-1

(To increase your understanding of various aspects of financial management)

1.  List the three major responsibilities of a financial manager.

    a.

    b.

    c.

2.  List the four principal terms of a commercial loan.

    a.

    b.

    c.

    d.

3.  Describe the two basic types of risk.

    a.

    b.

4.  List the three basic approaches to risk management.

    a.

    b.

    c.

EXERCISE 15-2

(To enhance your understanding of concepts related to insurance)

1. Why is insurance important for business firms?

2. List the three major classes of life insurance policies.

    a.

    b.

    c.

3. Briefly describe the types of insurance purchased by business firms.

    a.

    b.

    c.

    d.

    e.

    f.

    g.

    h.

    i.

    j.

    k.

4. Why are mortality tables important to insurance companies?

EXERCISE 15-3

(To strengthen your understanding of several basic financial concepts)

1.  Compare debt and equity financing in terms of repayment, claims on income, claims on assets, impact on management power, and taxes.

2.  Define net working capital.

3.  Fill in the blanks with the words "increased" or "decreased".

    a.  Accounts receivable are _____ by credit sales.

    b.  Cash (or the checking account) is _____ by cash sales.

    c.  Accounts payable are _____ by payments to creditors.

    d.  Accounts receivable are _____ by payments received from credit customers.

    e.  Accounts payable are _____ by credit purchases.

EXERCISE 15-4

(Scrambled Word Puzzle)

The letters for some of the key concepts from this chapter are scrambled on the left. Unscramble them and match each key concept with its definition somewhere in the right column.

A. ETRM

B. TFARD

C. UMTTYARI

D. KPUERRSI

E. LATIGNIKROWPAC

F. TYQIIILUD

G. TTIDERCEDAR

H. NNNOOLLPGARFI

I. FOENILTIDERC

J. STSOCYTINUTROPPO

1. There is no chance of gain

2. The factor of time of repayment

3. A firm's investment in short-term assets

4. The ability to make payments that are due

5. Cost of losing the option to use the funds in another way

6. Open book account

7. A special kind of secured financing

8. The bank stands ready to lend up to this amount to the borrower

9. An order to pay

10. These insurance policies are issued for definite time spans

EXERCISE 15-5

(Incident: A changing financial environment)

Answer the questions on a plain piece of paper.

The extremely high rate of inflation during the late 1970s made debt financing very attractive, especially long-term debt financing. Between 1975 and 1981, total corporate debt doubled. Business people were buying new equipment and other companies, and were expanding plants with borrowed money. They figured this was wise strategy because, due to inflation, they would be paying off the debt with dollars that had less and less purchasing power.

But in the early 1980s, many of those same firms were short on cash. The recession caused big slowdowns in inventory turnover, interest rates were very high, and cash flow problems were extremely critical.

Some financial managers expected that interest rates would have to come down or the economy would be crippled. Thus they shifted a growing volume of their borrowing to short-term loans, rather than committing their firms to high interest rates over a period of twenty or thirty years through the issuance of bonds. They turned more and more to commercial paper. In 1981, for example, the issuance of long-term bonds declined by about 20 percent while the issuance of commercial paper increased by about 33 percent.

Questions

1.  Discuss the liquidity of firms that are short on cash.

2.  What effect do cash shortages have on a firm's working capital?

3.  What effect do high interest rates have on the use of trade credit as a source of short-term funds?

4.  What effect do slowdowns in inventory turnover have on a firm's working capital?

5.  What are the advantages and disadvantages to a firm of reborrowing on commercial paper rather than issuing long-term bonds?

6.  Can a firm have too much short-term debt in relation to long-term debt? Explain.

CHAPTER 15 ANSWERS

Test Your Business Vocabulary

| | | |
|---|---|---|
| 1. | B | (pp. 440-441) |
| 2. | K | (p. 442) |
| 3. | L | (p. 447) |
| 4. | A | (p. 438) |
| 5. | M | (p. 439) |
| 6. | N | (p. 449) |
| 7. | H | (p. 455) |
| 8. | J | (p. 455) |

| | | |
|---|---|---|
| 9. | E | (p. 451) |
| 10. | C | (p. 448) |
| 11. | I | (p. 456) |
| 12. | Q | (p. 459) |
| 13. | P | (p. 458) |
| 14. | F | (p. 451) |
| 15. | O | (p. 449) |
| 16. | D | (p. 449) |

Programmed Review
(refer to the indicated pages
in the text)

1.
  A. (p. 438)
  B. (p. 438)
2.
  A. (p. 438)
  B. (p. 439)
  C. (p. 440)
3.
  A. (p. 441)
  B. (p. 441)
  C. (p. 441)
4.
  A. (p. 448)
  B. (p. 449)
  C. (p. 449)

5.
  A. (pp. 450-451)
  B. (p. 451)
6.
  A. (p. 454)
  B. (p. 453)
7.
  A. (p. 455)
  B. (p. 455)
8.
  A. (p. 456)
  B. (p. 456)
9.
  A. (p. 458)
  B. (p. 462)
  C. (p. 462)

Test Yourself (Multiple Choice)

1. C (p. 447)      6. D (p. 442)
2. B (p. 456)      7. B (p. 462)
3. A (p. 438)      8. C (p. 451)
4. C (p. 455)      9. D (pp. 441-442)
5. A (p. 449)     10. C (p. 453)

Test Yourself (True-False)

1. True (p. 440)     7. True (p. 455)
2. True (p. 440)     8. False (p. 461)
3. False (p. 447)    9. False (p. 448)
4. True (p. 449)    10. True (p. 459)
5. False (p. 459)
6. True (p. 451)

Exercise 15-1

1. (p. 438)
2. (p. 449)
3. (p. 455)
4. (pp. 453-454)

Exercise 15-4

A-10  term  (p. 462)
B- 9  draft (p. 451)
C- 2  maturity  (p. 440)
D- 1  pure risk  (p. 455)
E- 3  working capital
          (pp. 440-441)
F- 4  liquidity (p.442)
G- 6  trade credit (p. 448)
H- 7  floor planning (p. 449)
I- 8  line of credit (p. 449)
J- 5  opportunity costs
          (p. 447)

# CHAPTER 16

# The Securities Market and Long-Term Financing

At some point in the operation of a business, long-term capital will be needed. This capital may be invested in land, buildings, heavy machinery, and other fixed assets. This long-term capital is available in the public securities market by means of stock and bond issues. This chapter is designed to acquaint you with the fundamentals of long-term financing.

Stocks and bonds are the two primary vehicles by which a firm gains access to the public market. There are various types of stocks and bonds, each with advantages and disadvantages. Investment banks and brokerage houses are crucial institutions in the purchase and sale of stocks and bonds. To safeguard the interests of investors, securities operations are regulated by the Securities Exchange Commission.

The last section of the chapter covers extraordinary financing arrangements. These may include mergers, acquisitions, asset redeployment, recapitalization, and reorganization. These are financial alternatives that can be used depending upon the circumstances facing the organization.

# TEST YOUR BUSINESS VOCABULARY

Test your business vocabulary by matching each key concept with the proper phrase. Check your answers with those at the end of this chapter.

## Key Concepts

___ 1. bond
___ 2. investment bank
___ 3. brokerage house
___ 4. over-the-counter market
              (OTC)
___ 5. margin trading
___ 6. short selling
___ 7. lease
___ 8. sinking fund
___ 9. merger

___ 10. acquisition
___ 11. recapitalization
___ 12. reorganization
___ 13. mutual fund
___ 14. prospectus
___ 15. capital budget
___ 16. securities exchange

## Phrases

A. it includes information about the firm and the purpose of the proposed issue
B. a change in capital structure to reflect changing conditions internal or external to the firm
C. an involuntary process by which a court steps in to protect creditors from loss due to poor financial conditions in a firm
D. individual and institutional investors who buy stocks and bonds
E. a projection of expected needs for fixed assets over a five-to-ten year period
F. a certificate of indebtedness
G. it buys and sells on behalf of its investor-clients
H. it is also called an underwriting house
I. an agreement to grant use of an asset for a period of time in return for a periodic payment
J. a condition of insolvency combined with liabilities greater than assets
K. it is set aside over the lifetime of bonds for their retirement
L. successive renewals of short-term notes as a substitute for longer term commitments
M. an investment company
N. a complex of securities dealers who buy and sell securities for investors without using a securities exchange
O. a person who buys securities partly on credit financed by his/her stockbroker
P. the selling of a security that a person does not own by borrowing it from his broker
Q. places where buyers and sellers of securities deal with each other through members of the exchanges
R. the purchase by one firm of a controlling interest in another firm
S. two firms join together, or combine, to create a new firm
T. an intermediate term obligation similar to a bond, backed by

specific newly purchased assets

PROGRAMMED REVIEW

(To help you in understanding the chapter material and to see if you have mastered the objectives stated at the beginning of the chapter)

1. *Name several elements in the public securities market.*

   A. The two major vehicles by which a firm gains access to the public market are _____ and _____ .

   B. Most large- and medium-sized corporations use the public securities market as a source of _____ - _____ funds.

2. *Distinguish between several types of preferred stock.*

   A. With _____ _____ stock, shareholders are entitled only to the dividend stated on the stock certificate.

   B. With _____ _____ stock, shareholders can convert their preferred stock to common stock at their option.

3. *Explain what is meant by stock "value" and how this relates to stock dividends and stock splits.*

   A. The price the shares of stock are selling for on the market is known as _____ value.

   B. The value the corporation that originally issued the stock certificate may have printed on it is called _____ value.

   C. A _____ _____ gives stockholders a greater number of shares but does not change the individual's proportionate ownership in the corporation and it is not a dividend.

   D. A _____ dividend is a payment of cash to stockholders.

4. *Distinguish among several types of bonds.*

   A. With _____ bonds, the issuing corporation issues a large block of bonds which mature at different dates.

   B. _____ bonds are not backed by specific assets but are backed by the general credit and strength of the issuing corporation.

5. *Compare the services and functions of investment banks, brokerage houses, and securities exchanges.*

A.  A _____ _____ is a firm that buys and sells securities that previously have been issued by businesses and governments.

B.  An _____ _____ does not accept deposits from the general public, but it does help corporations to sell new issues of stocks and bonds.

C.  _____ _____ are set up by brokerage houses to reduce the cost and increase the efficiency of financial investment.

6.  *Translate a quote for a stock or bond as reported in The Wall Street Journal into dollar-and-cents terms.*

A.  A quote of 50 5/8 means that the price per share is $_____.

B.  Bond prices are expressed in terms of _____ even though most have a face or par value of $1,000.

7.  *Compare speculating with investing.*

A.  _____ trading means buying or selling securities in the hope of profiting from near-term future changes in their selling prices.

B.  An investor buys _____ for the longer haul.

8.  *Discuss the role of the Securities and Exchange Commission (SEC) in the securities market.*

A.  The SEC licenses brokerage houses and establishes _____ of conduct for them.

B.  A _____ is a summary of the registration statement that is filed with the SEC.

9.  *Explain the uses of long-term capital and capital budgeting.*

A.  Long term capital is invested in _____, _____, heavy machinery, and other fixed assets.

B.  The _____ _____ is based on expected sales growth and technology changes and projects capital needs for from five to twenty years.

10.  *Show how the sources of long-term capital differ between corporate and noncorporate firms.*

A.  Corporate long-term capital is available in the public securities market by means of _____ and _____ issues.

B.  When firms set aside money each year from profits to pay off bondholders, this is known as a _____ fund.

C. Sole proprietorships depend on the _____ funding of the owner-manager for equity financing.

11. *Present the advantages and possible disadvantages of leasing as an alternative to long-term financing of a purchase.*

A. A leasing arrangement _____ the outstanding debt of the firm.

B. There is often a _____ advantage to leasing because the entire lease payment is deductible.

C. A _____ is an agreement to grant use of an asset for a period of time in return for stated regular payments.

12. *Explain the special need for intermediate-term financing.*

A. Intermediate-term financing is for time periods greater than one year, but usually less than _____ years.

B. _____ _____ means successive renewals of short-term notes as a substitute for longer-term financial commitments.

13. *Show the relationship between mergers, acquisitions, and asset redeployment.*

A. In a _____, two firms join together, or combine, to create a new firm.

B. An _____ is the purchase by one firm of a controlling interest in another.

C. The action of selling company divisions is referred to as

_____ _____.

14. *Discuss the concepts of recapitalization, bankruptcy, and reorganization.*

A. _____ occurs when a firm changes its capital structure to meet changing conditions.

B. A firm that cannot meet its maturing financial obligations is

_____.

TEST YOURSELF (Multiple Choice)

Test yourself by selecting the best answer. Check your answers with those at the end of this chapter.

1. The value the corporation that originally issued the stock certificate may have printed on it is called:

   A. book value
   B. market value
   C. par value
   D. original value

2. Bonds not secured or backed by specific assets but by the general credit and strength of the issuing corporation are called:

   A. debenture bonds
   B. registered bonds
   C. coupon bonds
   D. serial bonds

3. A _____ market exists when stock prices as a whole are rising and there is a great deal of optimism among speculators.

   A. bear
   B. barren
   C. bolstering
   D. bull

4. A summary of the registration statement that is filed with the Securities Exchange Commission is called:

   A. a composite report
   B. a prospectus
   C. a status report
   D. an investment analysis

5. The selling of a security that a person does not own by borrowing it from his broker is called:

   A. short selling
   B. margin selling
   C. trade selling
   D. long selling

6. Which of the following is <u>not</u> an advantage of leasing assets?

   A. it is often a tax advantage
   B. leased equipment may be replaced without the losses that result from replacement of owned equipment
   C. it increases the outstanding debt of the firm

D.  a lease is usually a known, predictable cost factor

7.  When a firm is in very serious financial trouble and the court
    steps in to protect creditors, it is called:

    A.  recapitalization
    B.  acquisitions
    C.  asset redeployment
    D.  reorganization

8.  Which of the following is a way to reward stockholders when a firm
    wants to reinvest its earnings in the business?

    A.  stock split
    B.  stock dividends
    C.  cash dividends
    D.  cash split

9.  The Dow Jones Averages include all the following except:

    A.  the average of 30 industrial stocks
    B.  the average of 20 transportation stocks
    C.  the average of 15 stocks from nonprofit organizations
    D.  the average of 15 public utility stocks

10. Which of these is not accurate regarding the functions of large
    brokerage houses?

    A.  they perform a credit function
    B.  they perform an advisory function
    C.  they engage in investment banking
    D.  they do not perform a research function


TEST YOURSELF (True-False)

Test yourself by answering whether the following statements are true or
false.  Check your answers with those at the end of this chapter.

____  1.  Securities exchanges are set up by brokerage houses to reduce
          the cost and increase the efficiency of financial investment.

____  2.  A stock split gives stockholders fewer shares but does not
          change the individual's proportionate ownership in the corpora-
          tion.

____  3.  Investment banks accept deposits from the general public.

____  4.  The over-the-counter market is a complex of dealers who are
          in constant touch with one another.

____  5.  Blue-sky laws apply mainly to the sale of new securities.

_____ 6. Buying one share in a mutual fund makes you part-owner of all the securities owned by the fund.

_____ 7. Recapitalization occurs when a firm is in very serious financial trouble and the court steps in to protect creditors.

_____ 8. There are rarely tax advantages to leasing arrangements.

_____ 9. The difference between the dollar values of what a company owns and what it owes divided by the number of shares of common stock is called book value.

_____ 10. In a bear market, stock prices as a whole are rising.

EXERCISE 16-1

(To improve your understanding of stocks and bonds)

1. Briefly describe the three different concepts of value associated with common stock.

   a.


   b.


   c.


2. List the types of preferred stock.

   a.

   b.

   c.

   d.

   e.

   f.

3. Define the following terms:

   a.  stock split


   b.  cash dividend


   c.  stock dividend

4. List the nine basic types of bonds.

   a.

   b.

   c.

   d.

e.

f.

g.

h.

i.

EXERCISE 16-2

(To increase your understanding of various financing arrangements)

1.  Briefly explain the differences between recapitalization and re-
    organization.

2.  Why should decision-makers be concerned with antitrust laws when
    considering various forms of extraordinary financing arrangements?

3.  How do mergers differ from acquisitions?

4.  Compare and contrast voluntary and involuntary bankruptcy.

5.  Discuss some of the reasons that encourage firms to consider asset
    redeployment.

EXERCISE 16-3

(To improve your understanding of selected concepts related to the
securities market and long-term financing)

1. List the five basic functions that large brokerage houses perform
   for corporations and investors.

   a.

   b.

   c.

   d.

2. Distinguish between listed and unlisted securities.

3. What are the four basic advantages of leasing arrangements?

4. Define or describe the following terms.

   a. blue-sky laws

   b. prospectus

   c. capital budget

   d. sinking fund

   e. rolling over

EXERCISE 16-4

(Scrambled Word Puzzle)

The letters for some of the key concepts from this chapter are scrambled on the left.  Unscramble them and match each key concept with its definition somewhere in the right column.

A.  SEEAL

B.  ODNB

C.  PPSSTCEORU

D.  KYBNAPURCT

E.  NOITAZILATIPACER

F.  OOEULAVKB

G.  NOITAZINAGROER

H.  NIGARMRADTGNI

I.  PACILATDGUBET

J.  LLREVOGNIRO

K.  ORBREKEGAESUOH

L.  NUFDGNINIKS

1.  A change in capital structure to reflect changing conditions internal or external to the firm.

2.  It includes information about the firm and the purpose of the proposed issue.

3.  A certificate of indebtedness.

4.  A condition of insolvency combined with liabilities greater than assets.

5.  An agreement to grant use of an asset for a period of time in return for a periodic payment.

6.  An involuntary process by which a court steps in to protect creditors from loss due to poor financial conditions.

7.  Successive renewals of short-term notes as a substitute for longer term commitments.

8.  The difference between the dollar values of what a company owns and what it owes divided by the number of shares of common stock.

9.  It enables speculators to buy more shares for a given amount of money because they are buying partly on credit.

10.  A projection of expected needs for fixed assets over a five-to-ten year period.

11. Money set aside over the lifetime of bonds for their retirement.

12. A firm that buys and sells securities that previously have been issued by businesses and governments.

EXERCISE 16-5

(Incident:  A Common Stock Buy Back)

Answer the questions on a plain piece of paper.


In 1982 Warner Communications, Inc. filed with the Securities and Exchange Commission (SEC) details of a plan to buy back nearly ten percent of its outstanding common stock.  Management believed that this was a better investment than alternative investments because the market price of the stock was unrealistically low.  Warner planned to finance the buy back with short-term debt financing.

Warner owns Atari, which had made huge profits on its video games. Some investment advisers, however, were of the opinion that the video game bubble was bound to burst and if and when it did Warner's strong earnings performance would suffer.  Thus they were not recommending the purchase of Warner stock and its market price was falling.


Questions


1.  What factors basically determine the market value of shares of common stock?

2.  In addition to market value, what are two other concepts of value associated with common stock?  How are those values computed?

3.  Why do you think the Securities and Exchange Commission requires corporations that plan to buy back some of their outstanding common stock to file with the SEC?

4.  If you owned some Warner common stock, how would you feel about the buy back?  Explain.

5.  How might the buy-back program fit into any acquisition plans that Warner might have had?

Test Your Business Vocabulary

| | |
|---|---|
| 1. F (p. 471) | 9. S (p. 490) |
| 2. H (p. 472) | 10. R (p. 490) |
| 3. G (p. 472) | 11. B (p. 493) |
| 4. N (p. 476) | 12. C (p. 493) |
| 5. O (p. 479) | 13. M (p. 481) |
| 6. P (p. 480) | 14. A (p. 483) |
| 7. I (p. 488) | 15. E (p. 485) |
| 8. K (p. 487) | 16. Q (p. 474) |

Programmed Review
(refer to the indicated pages
in the text)

1.
  A. (p. 468)
  B. (p. 468)
2.
  A. (p. 469)
  B. (p. 469)
3.
  A. (p. 468)
  B. (p. 469)
  C. (p. 470)
  D. (p. 470)
4.
  A. (p. 471)
  B. (p. 471)
5.
  A. (p. 472)
  B. (p. 472)
  C. (p. 474)
6.
  A. (p. 476)
  B. (p. 477)

7.
  A. (p. 479)
  B. (p. 480)
8.
  A. (p. 483)
  B. (p. 483)
9.
  A. (P. 484)
  B. (p. 485)
10.
  A. (p. 486)
  B. (p. 487)
  C. (p. 488)
11.
  A. (p. 488)
  B. (p. 488)
  C. (p. 488)
12.
  A. (p. 489)
  B. (p. 489)
13.
  A. (P. 490)
  B. (p. 490)
  C. (p. 492)
14.
  A. (p. 493)
  B. (p. 493)

Exercise 16-1

1. (pp. 468-469)
2. (p. 469)
3. (pp. 469-470)
4. (p. 471)

Exercise 16-4

A-5  Lease (p. 488)
B-3  Bond (p. 471)
C-2  Prospectus (p. 483)
D-4  Bankruptcy (p. 493)
E-1  Recapitalization (p. 493)
F-8  Book value (p. 468)
G-6  Reorganization (p. 493)
H-9  Margin trading (p. 479)
I-10  Capital budget (p. 485)
J-7  Rolling over (p. 489)
K-12  Brokerage house (p. 472)
L-11  Sinking fund (p. 487)

Test Yourself (True-False)

1. True (p. 474)
2. False (p. 470)
3. False (p. 472)
4. True (p. 476)
5. True (p. 481)
6. True (p. 481)
7. False (p. 493)
8. False (p. 488)
9. True (p. 468
10. False (p. 479)

Test Yourself (Multiple Choice)

1. C (p. 469)
2. A (p. 471)
3. D (p. 479)
4. B (p. 483)
5. A (p. 480)
6. C (pp. 488-489)
7. D (p. 493)
8. B (p. 470)
9. C (p. 479)
10. D (p. 472)

# CHAPTER 17

# Small Business

Chapter 17 acquaints you with the opportunities and problems associated with small business operations. The operation of a small business is a dream for many people. One becomes a small business owner by taking over the family's business, buying out an existing firm or by starting a new firm. Each of these have varying degrees of attractiveness depending upon the individual's goals and the risks involved.

There are benefits and problems associated with small business ownership. The greatest single benefit is the sense of independence people feel from owning their firm. At the same time, there are numerous burdens. Small businesses require the full attention of owners and they are completely responsible for all problems that may be encountered.

Starting a small business requires time and effort. The process begins with careful planning of exactly what is to be accomplished. This planning process involves looking at financing, form of ownership, taxes, permits, insurance, and sources of information. Franchising has become a very popular method of going into business. Individuals should carefully evaluate the advantages and disadvantages of alternative franchise opportunities.

The U.S. government is keenly interested in small businesses. It developed the Small Business Administration to promote and protect the interests of small business firms. This agency provides numerous services, including management assistance, to strengthen small business operations.

# TEST YOUR BUSINESS VOCABULARY

Test your business vocabulary by matching each key concept with the proper phrase. Check your answers with those at the end of this chapter.

## Key Concepts

___ 1. small business
___ 2. venture capitalists
___ 3. economic development council
___ 4. franchising agreement
___ 5. Small Business Administration (SBA)
___ 6. SBA direct loans
___ 7. SBA participating loans
___ 8. SBA guaranteed loans
___ 9. Small Business Investment Company (SBIC)
___ 10. Small Business Institute (SBI)

## Phrases

A. individuals that are willing to provide equity capital to entrepreneurs who have new product ideas that are yet unproven, but potentially successful
B. a nonprofit organization of business firms that join together to help protect consumers and businesses from unfair business practices
C. a privately owned and privately operated company licensed by the SBA to help finance small firms for expansion and modernization
D. it was created in 1953 to promote and protect the interests of small business firms
E. these loans are made entirely with the SBA's own funds
F. a group of retired executives who volunteer their services to small firms that need management counseling
G. in this program, small business owners with problems are counseled by faculty and students from collegiate business schools
H. these loans supplement loans made from banks
I. SBA guarantees 90 percent of the loan
J. independently owned and operated for profit, not dominant in its field, and meets certain standards of size
K. a good source of data on the local economy
L. a contract between a franchiser and its franchisees

## PROGRAMMED REVIEW

(To help you in understanding the chapter material and to see if you have mastered the objectives stated at the beginning of the chapter)

1. *Explain, in your own words, the meaning of a "small business firm" and discuss the economic importance of small business in our*

*economic system.*

A. The SBA defines a small business as one that is _____ owned and operated for profit, not dominant in its field, and that meets certain standards of _____ in terms of employees or annual receipts.

B. Approximately _____ percent of American businesses are small businesses, and they account for about _____ percent of our gross national product.

2. *List and discuss three ways by which a person might become a small business owner.*

A. A person becomes a small business owner by taking over the family's business, by buying out an existing firm, or by starting a _____ firm.

B. The new entrepreneur has the opportunity to _____ the firm from the ground up.

3. *Discuss the nature of opportunity for small businesses.*

A. A small business is favored when customer _____ is more important than price and selection.

B. A small business is favored when a product does not lend itself to large-scale mass _____.

4. *Compare the benefits and burdens of entrepreneurship and assess your potential as a small business owner.*

A. The best thing about being your own boss is the sense of _____ you feel.

B. _____ is the major cause of business failures.

5. *List and discuss the first steps in starting your own business.*

A. Probably the most important step in starting a new business is estimating the amount of _____ needed to get started.

B. A good starting place in determining the financial needs is to draw up an overall _____ _____.

C. The main element in estimating cash inflows and cash outflows is _____.

6. *List and discuss the benefits of franchising to the two parties to a franchising agreement.*

   A. A franchiser enjoys widespread consumer _____ because the units are all basically alike.

   B. With respect to promotional assistance, a local franchisee pays a _____ rate for newspaper advertising than a national franchiser.

7. *Identify and describe the major types of programs sponsored by the Small Business Administration to aid small business.*

   A. _____ is a group of retired executives who volunteer their services to small firms that need management counseling.

   B. _____ is a privately owned and privately operated company licensed by the SBA to help finance small firms for expansion and modernization.

8. *Discuss minority-owned and women-owned small businesses.*

   A. A corporation is classified as women-owned if _____ percent or more of its stock is owned by women.

   B. Minority _____ _____ are government contracts that are awarded to minority-owned firms without competitive bidding.

TEST YOURSELF (Multiple Choice)

Test yourself by selecting the best answer. Check your answers with those at the end of this chapter.

1. A small business is:

   A. a firm that has sales less than one million dollars in a year
   B. hard to define in a way that is meaningful and satisfactory in all cases
   C. one that has fewer than 20 employees
   D. one that is owned by a single individual

2. Businesses police themselves through the:

   A. Small Business Administration
   B. Small Business Institute
   C. Better Business Bureau
   D. Economic Development Council

3. A franchisee can be thought of as:

A. an independent business owner
B. a person who licenses other people to sell his or her products or services
C. an employee of a franchiser
D. all of the above

4. Which of the following is <u>not</u> a drawback to franchising?

A. unscrupulous franchise promotors may be selling franchises that have little merit
B. there is little room for creativity because of uniformity of product and operations
C. there is less independence than you might expect
D. the franchiser is willing to live up to commitments in the franchising agreement

5. A Small Business Investment Company:

A. is owned and operated by the SBA
B. is licensed by the SBA
C. makes loans only to minority-owned firms
D. does not make loans to small firms but does provide them with equity capital

6. Individuals or businesses that are willing to provide equity capital to entrepreneurs who have new product ideas are called:

A. venture capitalists
B. equity experts
C. entrepreneurial capitalists
D. none of the above

7. All of the following are benefits of franchising to franchisers, except:

A. financial assistance
B. promotional assistance
C. diseconomies in buying
D. franchise recognition

8. SBA loans that supplement loans made from banks are called:

A. direct loans
B. guaranteed loans
C. partnership loans
D. participating loans

9. A group of active executives from all major industries and trade associations that volunteers its services to small business owners is:

A. SCORE
B. ACE
C. SBIC
D. MBDA

10. Which of the following certificates certifies that your type of business is permitted in that location under local zoning codes?

A. certificate of residence
B. certificate of zoning permission
C. certificate of location privilege
D. certificate of occupancy

TEST YOURSELF (True-False)

Test yourself by answering whether the following statements are true or false. Check your answers with those at the end of this chapter.

____ 1. A franchise is a firm that licenses other firms to sell its products.

____ 2. Venture capitalists seldom acquire a controlling interest in the firms they help to finance.

____ 3. Beginning entrepreneurs tend to underestimate sales revenues and overestimate costs.

____ 4. The Better Business Bureau (BBB) is a nonprofit organization of business firms that join together to help protect consumers and businesses from unfair business practices.

____ 5. To be considered a small business, a firm cannot have more than ten employees.

____ 6. The three basic types of SBA loans are direct, participating, and guaranteed.

____ 7. SBICs give the small business owner access to equity capital without the need to sell stock to the public.

____ 8. The main element in estimating cash inflows and cash outflows is timing.

____ 9. The SBA generally sponsors local economic development councils.

____ 10. Among the potential benefits of franchising to franchisees are diseconomies in buying and little management assistance.

EXERCISE 17-1

(To improve your understanding of various aspects of small business)

1. Discuss some examples of situations that tend to favor small firms.

2. List seven causes of business failures.

   a.

   b.

   c.

   d.

   e.

   f.

   g.

3. What are some of the benefits of entrepreneurship?

4. What are some of the burdens of entrepreneurship?

EXERCISE 17-2

(To help you determine if your personal characteristics are favorable or unfavorable to your becoming an entrepreneur)

Assume that you want to be an entrepreneur.  Place an X in the *Yes* column if the phrase on the left describes one of your personal characteristics or attitudes.  Otherwise, place a X in the *No* column. Circle those Xs that you think indicate a necessary characteristic or attitude of an entrepreneur.

|  |  | *Yes* | *No* |
|---|---|---|---|
| 1. | I want to have plenty of free time. | ___ | ___ |
| 2. | I get along well with other people. | ___ | ___ |
| 3. | I do not like to be responsible for getting results. | ___ | ___ |
| 4. | I usually get things done if someone gives me a little push. | ___ | ___ |
| 5. | You show me what you want done and I will do it. | ___ | ___ |
| 6. | I am a self-starter. | ___ | ___ |
| 7. | I like to plan but I do not like to work hard to reach my goals. | ___ | ___ |
| 8. | The most important thing to me is security.  I do not like risk. | ___ | ___ |
| 9. | I can take stress and pressure. | ___ | ___ |
| 10. | If I do not succeed on the first try, I will try again. | ___ | ___ |
| 11. | I do not make decisions until I have *all* the facts. | ___ | ___ |
| 12. | I am able to learn from my mistakes. | ___ | ___ |
| 13. | I believe that I can do everything better than anybody else. | ___ | ___ |

EXERCISE 17-3

(To acquaint you with selected aspects of starting a small business)

1.  List three examples of licenses and permits that may be needed to enter a small business.

    a.

    b.

    c.

2.  List three common types of taxes that must be paid by small businesses.

    a.

    b.

    c.

3.  Describe  the type of information that can be acquired from the following sources.

    a.  Better Business Bureau

    b.  Chamber of Commerce

    c.  economic development council

4.  List five benefits of franchising to franchisees.

    a.

    b.

    c.

    d.

    e.

5. Briefly describe the three basic types of SBA loans.

    a.

    b.

    c.

EXERCISE 17-4

(Scrambled Word Puzzle)

The letters for some of the key concepts from this chapter are scrambled on the left. Unscramble them and match each key concept with its definition somewhere in the right column. Finally, the letters in parentheses in the *unscrambled* key concepts form another key concept. What is it? In this exercise, abbreviations such as SBA may be used as scrambled words.

A. RESCO　　　　　_ (_) _ _ _

B. NARFISERCH　　_ _ _ _ _ _ (_) _ _ _

C. NATARUGDEE　　_ _ _ _ _ (_) (_) _ _ _

D. CISB　　　　　_ _ (_) _

E. BSI　　　　　_ _ (_)

F. TENERERNERUP　_ _ (_) _ _ (_) _ _ _ _ _ _

G. ERDICT ANOLS　_ _ (_) _ _ _ _ _ (_) _ _

H. EECHIFARNS　　_ _ (_) _ _ _ _ _ _ _

I. _ _ _ _ _ _ _ _ P _ _ _ _ G LOANS

1. Loans made to entrepreneurs with SBA funds and with funds from private sources

2. A person or firm licensed to sell a francisher's products in a specific territory

3. A loan which the SBA has agreed to cover (up to 90%) in the event of default

4. Licenses franchisees to sell its products in specified territories

5. Loans made to entrepreneurs entirely with SBA funds

6. Provides counseling to small business owners by faculty and students at college

7. Members of this SBA advisory service are retired

executives who
volunteer their
services to aid
small firms with
management problems

8. Licensed by the SBA
   to provide long-term
   financing to small
   business firms

9. A person who assumes
   the risk of organi-
   zing and running a
   business in the hope
   of making a profit

EXERCISE 17-5

(Incident: What is a small business?)

Answer the questions on a plain piece of paper.


The Small Business Act of 1953 broadly defines a small business as one that is independently owned and not dominant in its field. The act, however, also authorizes the administrator of the Small Business Administration (SBA) to establish more specific, industry-related criteria that can be used in determining eligibility for the various types of SBA programs and assistance.

In 1978 the SBA began a major study of its size standards. As a result of that study, the SBA has announced its intention to propose major revisions. Thus on March 10, 1980 the SBA issued its first advance notice of proposed size standard revisions. This was followed on May 3, 1982 by a second advance notice of proposed size standard revisions.

As Chapter 17 of the text points out, the SBA has traditionally used a variety of measures for size determination. The May 3, 1982 notice referred to above uses one criterion for measuring business size--number of employees--but retains the annual receipts criterion for measuring business size in agriculture and construction. Measuring employment in the agriculture industry raises the issue of whether family members and relatives are considered employees. In the construction industry, the problem is whether employees of subcontractors should be included in the employee count.

Questions

1. Why is the SBA's definition of "small business" so important?

2. Do you think the SBA should consider the form of ownership of a firm in determining SBA size standards? For example, should the number of employees standard for a corporation be higher than that for a sole proprietorship? Why or why not?

3. Do you think the SBA should revise the number of employees standard that it indicated in its May 3, 1982 notice? Explain.

Test Your Business
Vocabulary

1. J (p. 504)    6. E (p. 525)
2. A (p. 513)    7. H (p. 525)
3. K (p. 516)    8. I (p. 525)
4. L (p. 519)    9. C (p. 526)
5. D (p. 524)   10. G (p. 527)

Programmed Review
(refer to the indicated pages
in the text)

1.                    5.
   A. (p. 504)           A. (p. 511)
   B. (p. 504)           B. (p. 512)
2.                       C. (p. 512)
   A. (p. 505)        6.
   B. (p. 507)           A. (p. 519)
3.                       B. (p. 521)
   A. (p. 507)        7.
   B. (p. 507)           A. (p. 527)
4.                       B. (p. 526)
   A. (p. 509)        8.
   B. (p. 510)           A. (p. 527)
                         B. (p. 529)

Test Yourself (Multiple Choice)

1. B (p. 504)    6. A (p. 513)
2. C (p. 516)    7. C (p. 519)
3. A (p. 519)    8. D (p. 525)
4. D (p. 524)    9. B (p. 527)
5. B (p. 526)   10. D (p. 515)

Test Yourself (True-False)

1. False (p. 519)
2. False (p. 513)
3. False (p. 513)
4. True (p. 516)
5. False (pp. 504-505)
6. True (p. 524)
7. True (p. 526)
8. True (p. 512)
9. False (p. 516)
10. False (p. 519)

Exercise 17-3

1. (pp. 514-515)
2. (p. 515)
3. (p. 516)
4. (p. 519)
5. (p. 525)

Exercise 17-4

A.  SCORE (7) (p. 527)
B.  Franchiser (4) (p. 519)
C.  Guaranteed (3) (p. 525)
D.  SBIC (8) (p. 526)
E.  SBI (6) (p. 526)
F.  Entrepreneur (9) (p. 509)
G.  Direct loans (5) (p. 525)
H.  Franchisee (2) (p. 519)
I.  Participating loans (1)
                    (p. 525)

# CHAPTER 18

# International Business

Chapter 18 is the first attempt to acquaint you with business operations beyond the United States. International business creates new types of business opportunity and stimulates international contact.

International business allows for broadening the scope of the market and makes greater exchange and specialization possible. Countries have advantages in certain product areas, both absolute and comparative. This is important in helping nations focus their efforts.

International trade does not take place without some barriers. Some of these barriers are natural, tariff, and other created barriers. These barriers are obstacles that restrict trade among countries.

Two additional concepts that are important in understanding international trade are balance of trade and balance of payments. A nation's balance of trade is the difference between the money values of its exports and its imports. The balance of payments is the difference between a country's receipt of foreign money and the outflows of its own money. These concepts are important in understanding the importance of international trade to the United States.

Exporting and importing are types of involvement in international business. Firms make the decision to export to get the cost-per-unit down to a low level, to combat the problems of reaching the decline stage of the product life cycle, and to enhance profits. Firms import to supplement domestic sources.

The final section focuses on the multinational business environment. Included are the sociocultural, economic, technological, and political and legal environments.

# TEST YOUR BUSINESS VOCABULARY

Test your business vocabulary by matching each key concept with the proper phrase.  Check you answers with those at the end of the chapter.

## Key Concepts

| | |
|---|---|
| ___ 1. international trade | ___ 10. cartel |
| ___ 2. absolute advantage | ___ 11. piggyback exporting |
| ___ 3. tariffs | ___ 12. expropriation |
| ___ 4. embargo | ___ 13. foreign licensing |
| ___ 5. dumping | ___ 14. joint venture |
| ___ 6. General Agreement on Tariffs and Trade (GATT) | ___ 15. multinational company |
| | ___ 16. foreign exchange rate |
| ___ 7. comparative advantage | ___ 17. import quota |
| ___ 8. balance of trade | ___ 18. trade barriers |
| ___ 9. balance of payments | |

## Phrases

A. the reason why a country that can produce all goods better than any other country can still benefit from foreign trade

B. goods that enter a country from other countries

C. obstacles that restrict trade among nations

D. taxes that a government puts on products imported into or exported from a country

E. places a limit on the amount of a product that can enter a country

F. prohibits the import and/or export of certain products into or out of a country

G. government control over access to its country's currency by foreigners

H. it tells how much a unit of one currency is worth in terms of a unit of another

I. the difference between the money values of its exports and its imports

J. a group of business firms or nations that agree to operate as a monopoly

K. a firm based in one country and has production and marketing activities spread in one or more foreign countries

L. the government of a country takes over ownership of a foreign-owned firm located in its country

M. a group of countries that agree to eliminate barriers to trade among member nations

N. a partnership of two or more partners that are based in different countries

O. the difference between a country's receipts of foreign money and the outflows of its own money

P. selling goods abroad at prices lower than full cost

Q. flows of goods between or among nations

R. only or cheapest producer has this

S. treaty among major trading nations

243

T.  one firm uses its overseas distribution network to sell noncom-
    petitive products made by another firm
U.  a firm in one country gives a firm in another country the right
    to use the licensor's patent, trademark, etc., in return for an
    agreed-upon percentage of sales revenues


PROGRAMMED REVIEW

(To help you in understanding the chapter material and to see if you
have mastered the objectives stated at the beginning of the chapter)

1.  *Explain why international trade is beneficial to the nations that
    trade.*

    A.  A country enjoys an _____ advantage in producing a pro-
        duct when either (1) it is the only country that can provide
        it, or (2) it can produce it at a lower cost than any other
        country.

    B.  International trade involves the _____ of goods and
        services between one country and other countries.

2.  *Differentiate between state and private trading companies.*

    A.  A state trading company is a _____-owned operation that
        handles a country's trade with other governments or firms in
        other countries.

    B.  A private trading company is a privately owned business that
        _____ and _____ goods in many different countries.

3.  *Identify and give examples of the various types of barriers to
    international trade.*

    A.  The three categories of trade barriers are _____ barriers,
        _____ barriers, and other created barriers.

    B.  An _____ prohibits the import and/or export of certain
        products into or out of a country.

    C.  _____ control means government control over access to its
        country's currency by foreigners.

4.  *Give examples of how the United States government aids American
    firms in conducting international business.*

    A.  Governments can help to promote trade by reducing or removing
        trade _____.

B. One of the most important multilateral agreements is the GATT, which stands for _____ _____ on _____ and _____.

5. *Distinguish between a country's balance of trade and its balance of payments.*

   A. The balance of trade is the difference between the money values of a nation's _____ and _____.

   B. A country's _____ of _____ is the difference between its receipts of foreign money and the outflows of its own money.

6. *Discuss the effects of fluctuating foreign exchange rates on international trade.*

   A. The foreign exchange rate is the _____ of one currency to another.

   B. Exchange rates can _____ from day to day, and this adds an additional element of risk to international business.

7. *Give reasons why firms import and export products.*

   A. Firms may export for reasons related to the product _____ cycle.

   B. Importing is necessary in the case of oil because domestic sources must be _____ by foreign sources.

8. *Identify and discuss the major tasks an exporter faces in exporting goods from the United States.*

   A. A shipper's _____ declaration is required for all goods exported from the United States.

   B. In _____ exporting, a manufacturer uses its overseas distribution network to sell noncompetitive products of one or more other firms.

9. *Compare exporting and foreign operations as strategies for entering foreign markets.*

   A. A multinational company is a firm based in one country and has _____ and _____ activities spread in one or more foreign countries.

   B. In a _____ _____ agreement, a firm in one country gives a firm in another country the right to use the licensor's patent, trademark, copyright, technology, processes,

245

and/or products in return for an agreed-upon percentage of the licensee's sales revenues or profits resulting from such use.

10. *List and discuss several important environmental factors that affect multinational business.*

    A. A country's tax structure is considered part of the _____ environment.

    B. The _____ environment would include such things as language and values.


TEST YOURSELF (Multiple Choice)

Test yourself by selecting the best answer. Check your answers with those at the end of this chapter.

1. If a country's balance of trade is favorable, its balance of payments:

    A. will also be favorable
    B. will have a surplus
    C. cannot be unfavorable
    D. can be favorable or unfavorable

2. A multinational firm:

    A. exports a large volume of manufactured goods from its home country
    B. conducts most of its international business through export agents
    C. has production and marketing operations in one or more host countries
    D. engages mainly in indirect exporting

3. Which of the following is a natural barrier to trade?

    A. distance
    B. tax control
    C. customs procedures
    D. import quotas

4. A group of business firms or nations that agree to operate as a monopoly is called:

    A. an oligopoly
    B. an economic system
    C. a cartel
    D. a monopsony

5. Government control over access to its country's currency by foreigners is known as:

   A. exchange control
   B. currency control
   C. monetary control
   D. economic control

6. Which of the following does not accurately describe a bill of lading?

   A. it is a document of title that can be transferred after endorsement
   B. it is a contract between the shipper and the transportation company
   C. it is a receipt for the goods the shipper has placed on the carrier
   D. it is a type of insurance coverage

7. When firms from a host country and a foreign country engage in a co-owned business which operates in the host country, you have a:

   A. joint venture
   B. licensing arrangement
   C. contract manufacturing agreement
   D. foreign assembly plant

8. A major purpose of a regional trading bloc is to:

   A. reduce the volume of trade among member countries
   B. expand trade with nonmember countries
   C. make each member country self-sufficient
   D. eliminate trade barriers among member countries

9. Which of the following is a treaty through which member countries act jointly to reduce trade barriers?

   A. FCIA
   B. SBA
   C. GATT
   D. CEM

10. _____ means shipping substantial quantities of a product to a foreign country at prices that are below either the home-market price of the same product or the full cost of producing it.

   A. Dropping
   B. Dumping
   C. Unloading
   D. Expropriation

TEST YOURSELF (True-False)

Test yourself by answering whether the following statements are true or false. Check you answers with those at the end of this chapter.

___  1.  Distance is a major natural barrier to international trade.

___  2.  An import quota places a limit on the amount of a product that can leave a country.

___  3.  Countries that practice tax control are more likely to attract foreign investment than countries that do not practice it.

___  4.  International trade allows each country to use its scarce resources more economically.

___  5.  Government regulations concerning safety and health and other product standards can serve as nontariff barriers.

___  6.  A nation's balance of payments is the difference between the money values of its exports and its imports.

___  7.  In piggyback exporting, a manufacturer uses its overseas distribution network to sell noncompetitive products of one or more other firms.

___  8.  A multinational company is a firm based in one country and has production and marketing activities spread in one or more foreign countries.

___  9.  Expropriation means that the government of a country takes over ownership of a locally-owned firm.

___  10.  The European Common Market is an example of a regional trading bloc.

EXERCISE 18-1

(To enhance your understanding of barriers to international trade and governmental assistance to international business)

1. What are natural barriers to international trade?

2. What are the two main purposes of tariffs?

   a.

   b.

3. List the eight basic types of created, nontariff barriers.

   a.

   b.

   c.

   d.

   e.

   f.

   g.

   h.

4. Discuss the purpose of the General Agreement on Tariffs and Trade (GATT).

5. Briefly describe the purpose of the following institutions:

a. Export-Import Bank

b. International Monetary Fund

c. International Development Association

d. Foreign Trade Zones

EXERCISE 18-2

(To improve your understanding of selected aspects of international business)

1. "A nation with a favorable balance of trade can have an unfavorable balance of payments."  Explain this statement.

2. List five common reasons why firms export products.

   a.

   b.

   c.

   d.

   e.

3. Define the following terms or concepts:

   a.  piggyback exporting

   b.  foreign freight forwarder

   c.  shipper's export declaration

   d.  validated export license

4. Differentiate between comparative advantage and absolute advantage.

5. List the four basic arguments for tariffs.

   a.


   b.



   c.



   d.

EXERCISE 18-3

(To enhance your understanding of specific issues regarding international business operations)

1.  What effects do fluctuating exchange rates have on international trade?




2.  List the various multinational business environments that one must consider.

    a.

    b.

    c.

    d.

3.  Contrast state and private trading companies.




4.  List the most common methods of handling payment by the importer to the exporter:

    a.

    b.

    c.

    d.

EXERCISE 18-4

(Word Puzzle)

Arranged in a column below is one of the key concepts from this chapter. Opposite each letter of this key concept is the definition of another key concept also found in this chapter. Fill in the blanks provided with the remaining letter of the defined key concept.

_ _ B _ _ _ _              1. Legal prohibition placed on trade with a particular country

_ A _ _ _ _                2. A group of firms that agrees to act as a monopoly

_ _ _ L _ _ _ _ _ _        3. Required for all goods exported from the United States; a shipper's export _____

_ A _ _ _ _ _              4. Taxes on imported or exported goods

_ _ _ N _ _ _ _ _ _ _ _    5. An arrangement with a foreign firm which results in a mutual ownership of a firm

_ _ C _ _ _ _ _            6. The process of converting one currency into another

_ _ _ E _ _ _ _ _          7. Granting of permission for someone to make and sell your products overseas

_ O _ _ _ _ _ _ _ _        8. A type of advantage every country enjoys in something

F _ _ _ _ _ _              9. Not domestic; outside the country

_ _ _ _ _ T _ _ _ _ _      10. A government company engaging in international trade

_ _ _ _ R _ _ _ _ _ _ _    11. Between countries; a type of trade

_ _ _ _ _ _ A _ _ _ _ _    12. A company which is a global enterprise

D _ _ _ _ _ _          13. Selling a product in a for-
                            eign market at prices below
                            the full cost of producing
                            it

_ _ _ _ _ E _ _        14. Obstacles to foreign trade

EXERCISE 18-5

(Incident: Reciprocity in International Business)

Answer the questions on a plain piece of paper.


Several bills were introduced in Congress in 1982 that had one element in common--reciprocity in international trade. In this case, reciprocity means treating other nations as they treat the United States with respect to trade barriers. Thus, if a country imposes trade barriers that hurt American-based firms exporting to or doing business in that country, the United States would reciprocate by imposing its own barriers against trade with that country.

Meanwhile, an increasing volume of international trade is being conducted on a reciprocal basis. In this case, reciprocity is tied to the practice of barter. For example, the government of a country may allow the import of a given product only if the foreign exporter will accept payment in goods produced in that country. Barter replaces money and credit as the medium of exchange in these international transactions.

Questions

1. Is there any difference between "protectionism" and "reciprocity", as reciprocity is defined in the first paragraph above? Explain.

2. Does a country that effectively closes its market through trade barriers to goods coming from a country to which it exports really view international trade as a two-way street? Explain.

3. Refer to the discussion of mercantilism on page 15 of the text. Is mercantilist philosophy evident in a country that wants to build its exports while limiting its imports? Explain.

4. Are reciprocal trading deals as described in the second paragraph above a type of restriction on international trade? Why or why not?

# CHAPTER 18 ANSWERS

## Test Your Business Vocabulary

| | | |
|---|---|---|
| 1. Q (p. 534) | 7. A (p. 534) | 13. U (p. 558) |
| 2. R (p. 534) | 8. I (p. 545) | 14. N (p. 558) |
| 3. D (p. 538) | 9. O (p. 545) | 15. K (p. 554) |
| 4. F (p. 540) | 10. J (p. 556) | 16. H (p. 548) |
| 5. P (pp. 543-544) | 11. T (pp. 553-554) | 17. E (p. 539) |
| 6. S (p. 544) | 12. L (p. 556) | 18. C (p. 537) |

## Programmed Review
(refer to the indicated pages in the text)

1.
   A. (p. 534)
   B. (p. 534)
2.
   A. (p. 536)
   B. (p. 536)
3.
   A. (p. 537)
   B. (p. 540)
   C. (p. 541)
4.
   A. (p. 544)
   B. (p. 544)
5.
   A. (p. 545)
   B. (p. 545)

6.
   A. (p. 548)
   B. (p. 548)
7.
   A. (p. 549)
   B. (p. 549)
8.
   A. (p. 550).
   B. (pp. 553-554)
9.
   A. (p. 554)
   B. (p. 558)
10.
   A. (pp. 559-560)
   B. (p. 559)

## Test Yourself (Multiple Choice)

| | |
|---|---|
| 1. D (p. 545) | 6. D (p. 551) |
| 2. C (p. 554) | 7. A (p. 558) |
| 3. A (p. 538) | 8. D (p. 556) |
| 4. C (p. 556) | 9. C (p. 544) |
| 5. A (p. 541) | 10. B (pp. 543-544) |

## Test Yourself (True-False)

| | |
|---|---|
| 1. True (p. 538) | 6. False (p. 545) |
| 2. False (p. 539) | 7. True (pp. 553-554) |
| 3. False (p. 541) | 8. True (p. 554) |
| 4. True (p. 534) | 9. False (p. 556) |
| 5. True (p. 541) | 10. True (p. 556) |

## Exercise 18-4

1. embargo (p. 540)
2. cartel (p. 556)
3. declaration (p. 550)
4. tariffs (p. 538)
5. joint venture (p. 558)
6. exchange (p. 540)
7. licensing (p. 558)
8. comparative (p. 534)
9. foreign (p. 548)
10. state trading (p. 536)
11. international (p. 534)
12. multinational (p. 554)
13. dumping (pp. 543-544)
14. barriers (p. 537)

## Exercise 18-1

1. (p. 538)
2. (p. 538)
3. (pp. 538-539)
4. (p. 544)
5. (pp. 542-543) (Table 18-4)

# CHAPTER 19

# Government and Business

Managers make decisions in an environment that can make the difference between success and failure. Among the relevant environmental influences are government, society, and technology. These environments are dynamic and interdependent.

One of the most potent of the environmental influences is the government. Numerous laws and regulations restrict, limit, or impact on business operations. The law expects firms to compete, to provide tax revenues, and to serve the consumer fairly. These expectations are clearly outlined in antitrust laws (such as the Sherman and Clayton Acts), consumer protection laws (such as the Consumer Product Safety Act) and others. In addition to its role as regulator, government plays the roles of competitor, economic stabilizer, supporter, customer, and "housekeeper."

In order to facilitate the smooth flow of business operations, business law concepts must be understood. Some of the concepts and institutions presented in this chapter are the law of contracts, the law of agency and bailments, the law of property, and the Uniform Commercial Code. Managers must be aware of and understand the judicial-legal aspects of government's impact on business.

TEST YOUR BUSINESS VOCABULARY

Test your business vocabulary by matching each key concept with the proper phrase. Check your answers with those at the end of this chapter.

Key Concepts

___ 1. administrative law
___ 2. consent order
___ 3. antitrust laws
___ 4. progressive tax
___ 5. regressive tax
___ 6. common law

___ 7. statutory law
___ 8. contract
___ 9. Uniform Commercial Code (UCC)
___ 10. agency-principal relationship
___ 11. real property
___ 12. personal property

Phrases

A. the firm agrees to accept deregulation
B. they try to get firms to compete against each other
C. the federal income tax is an example
D. built on precedents, or the previous opinions of judges
E. land and its permanent attachments
F. a legal promise made by the seller that assures the buyer that the product is or shall be as represented by the seller
G. all states except Louisiana have adopted it
H. furniture, clothing, cars, and bank accounts
I. poorer people pay a higher percent of their income than richer people
J. this law is written or codified by city councils, state legislatures, or Congress
K. a mutual agreement between two or more people to perform or not perform certain acts
L. when one party is authorized and consents to act on behalf of another
M. government officials act both as judges and as legislators
N. an agreement to "cease and desist" a practice


PROGRAMMED REVIEW

(To help you in understanding the chapter material and to see if you have mastered the objectives stated at the beginning of the chapter)

1. *Show how business creates part of the environment of society.*

   A. The _____ of something consists of all those things that come in contact with it and influence it.

   B. The closing of a plant in a town demonstrates how business is an important part of _____ environment.

2. *Explain how environmental influences are interdependent.*

   A. Environmental influences are interdependent in that a change in one environment usually results in a _____ in all of the others.

   B. There is a kind of _____ reaction between and among environmental influences.

3. *Give an example of at least three different roles played by government in the environment of business.*

   A. Amtrak and TVA are examples of the government being a _____ of private business.

   B. The Small Business Administration is an example of the government being a _____ of private business.

   C. As a defense system, government is a _____ of business.

4. *Name and describe the purpose of several federal administrative and regulatory agencies.*

   A. The _____ _____ _____ issues trade practice rules and trade regulation rules.

   B. The _____ and _____ _____ prohibits adulteration and misbranding of foods, drugs, devices, and cosmetics.

5. *Explain the nature of antitrust activity.*

   A. Antitrust laws try to get firms to _____ against each other.

   B. The _____ _____ Act was the first of the general antitrust laws.

6. *Explain the concept of deregulation and its cause.*

   A. The first mode of transportation to be _____ was the airlines.

   B. It has been estimated that the total cost of regulation to American business is over $_____ billion each year.

7. *Differentiate between regressive and progressive taxes.*

   A. A _____ tax makes richer people pay a higher percent of their income than poorer people.

   B. A _____ tax means that poorer people pay a higher percent of their income than richer people.

8. *List and define the parts of a valid contract.*

   A. In order to be valid, a contract must include an agreement,

      _____ , _____ , and a legal objective.

   B. The value that each party gets or gives in a contractual relationship is known as _____ .

9. *Discuss the basic ideas of agency and bailment.*

   A. An agency-_____ relationship exists when one party is authorized and consents to act on behalf of another.

   B. In a bailor-bailee relationship, the _____ gives possession

      and control of his or her property to the _____ .

10. *Outline the main points in the law of property.*

    A. Land and its permanent attachments are known as _____ property.

    B. All property other than real property is known as _____ property.

11. *Explain the significance of the Uniform Commercial Code to business.*

    A. The Uniform Commercial Code (UCC) is a _____ that combines and coordinates uniform acts into a single commercial code.

    B. All states except _____ have adopted the UCC.

    C. The UCC reduces the problems firms face in _____ commerce.

TEST YOURSELF (Multiple Choice)

Test yourself by selecting the best answer. Check your answers with those at the end of this chapter.

1. The first of the federal antitrust laws was:

   A. the Sherman Act
   B. the Clayton Act
   C. the Grant Law
   D. the Robinson-Patman Act

2. A tax which causes poorer people to pay a higher percentage of their income than richer people is a:

   A. progressive tax
   B. value added tax
   C. regressive tax
   D. property tax

3. At the national level, the law expects firms to do all of the following except:

   A. compete
   B. maximize profits
   C. provide tax revenues
   D. serve the consumer fairly

4. The value that each party gets or gives in a contractual relationship is known as:

   A. consolation
   B. money
   C. property
   D. consideration

5. Land (and its permanent attachments, such as houses, garages, and office buildings) is also called:

   A. personal property
   B. legal property
   C. real property
   D. common property

6. Which class of law is built on precedents?

   A. common law
   B. administrative law
   C. statutory law
   D. sales law

7. The government plays many roles with respect to business. When considering the Federal Trade Commission (FTC), which of the following roles is the government performing?

   A. competitor
   B. supporter
   C. customer
   D. regulator

8. Which of the following is not one of "the basic rights of consumers" as proclaimed by President Kennedy in the 1960s?

A. the right to choose
B. the right to compete
C. the right to be informed
D. the right to safety

9. Which state has <u>not</u> adopted the Uniform Commercial Code (UCC)?

   A. Louisiana
   B. Vermont
   C. Florida
   D. Washington

10. In an agency-principal relationship, the person who acts on behalf of another person is the:

   A. bailor
   B. bailee
   C. principal
   D. agent

TEST YOURSELF (True-False)

Test yourself by answering whether the following statements are true or false. Check your answers with those at the end of this chapter.

____ 1. The UCC is a statute that combines and coordinates uniform acts into a single commercial code.

____ 2. The law of contracts is basic to the right to own property.

____ 3. Voluntary compliance means that the firm agrees to do what the agency advises after a hearing is held.

____ 4. The federal income tax is an example of a regressive tax.

____ 5. Antitrust laws try to get firms to stop competing.

____ 6. The U.S. Government at times plays the role of competitor of private business, supporter of private business, or customer of business.

____ 7. Under administrative law, government officials act both as judges and as legislators.

____ 8. One of the basic tenets of supply side economics is that government should concentrate on encouraging business to grow and expand.

____ 9. Very little opposition exists when deregulation efforts are undertaken by the federal government.

___ 10. The federal government is the single largest buyer of goods and services in the nation.

EXERCISE 19-1

(To help you understand the roles of government with respect to business)

1. Briefly describe the various roles of government with respect to business.

    a.

    b.

    c.

    d.

    e.

    f.

2. State the purpose of the following administrative and regulatory agencies.

    a.  Interstate Commerce Commission (ICC)

    b.  Federal Trade Commission (FTC)

    c.  Environmental Protection Agency (EPA)

    d.  Food and Drug Administration (FDA)

    e.  Consumer Product Safety Commission (CPSC)

3. The environments of business, government, society, and technology are dynamic and interdependent." Do you agree or disagree? Explain.

EXERCISE 19-2

(To improve your understanding of antitrust considerations)

1.  What is the underlying purpose of all antitrust laws?

2.  What is laissez faire and how does it differ from the existing role of government?

3.  Briefly state the major purpose of each of the following pieces of antitrust legislation:

    a.  Sherman Act of 1890

    b.  Clayton Act of 1914

    c.  Federal Trade Commission Act of 1914

    d.  Robinson-Patman Act of 1936

    e.  Wheeler-Lea Act of 1938

    f.  Celler-Kefauver Act of 1950

EXERCISE 19-3

(To better acquaint you with business law concepts and institutions)

1.  List the two broad classes of law.

    a.

    b.

2.  List the four elements of a valid contract.

    a.

    b.

    c.

    d.

3.  Discuss the nature of the agency-principal relationship and give an example.

4.  Discuss the nature of the bailor-bailee relationship.

5.  List and give examples of the two main types of property.

    a.

    b.

6. List the types of real property ownership:

    a.

    b.

    c.

    d.

    e.

    f.

7. Why is the UCC important?

EXERCISE 19-4

(Scrambled Word Puzzle)

The letters for some of the key concepts from this chapter are scrambled on the left. Unscramble them and match each key concept with its definition somewhere in the right column.

A. LIABEMTN

B. TTTNAIUSR

C. NULOVRTYA

D. NOINOCTAREDIS

E. ESTNOCN

F. CUC

G. PPRREEOYTRLA

H. EVISGORPSER

I. RRRSSXEPEYTWAAN

J. INIMDAEVITARTS

1. Laws designed to maintain competition.

2. A tax which places the burden of payment more heavily on the highly paid.

3. Law under which FTC and similar government agencies act as judges and legislators.

4. Agreement to comply with regulations when found in violation without formal proceedings.

5. A transfer of possession without sale.

6. The value that each party gets and gives in a contractual relationship.

7. Land is an example.

8. A specific representation that is made by the seller.

9. A statute that combines and coordinates uniform acts into a single commercial code.

10. The order whereby a firm found to be engaging in a questionable practice agrees to quit the practice.

EXERCISE 19-5

(Incident: The Flat-rate Tax)

Answer the questions on a plain piece of paper.


Many people in the United States are talking about a flat-rate federal income tax. Proponents claim that such a tax would be easier and less costly to administer than the current progressive federal income tax. Thus, if the rate were set at 20 percent, everyone would pay 20 percent of gross income to the federal government.

People who favor the flat-rate tax say it would be more equitable. The rich would not be able to avoid paying their fair share of taxes by hiring tax experts to find loopholes. Taxpayers would also have a harder time cheating and a much easier task of preparing their income tax returns. Advocates also contend it would reduce the problem of "bracket creep" (see the incident, Indexing Federal Income Taxes, on page 59 of the text) and erase the marriage penalty. (The marriage penalty is incurred when spouses combine their incomes and, as a result, move into a higher bracket.) Finally, people who favor the flat-rate tax say it would improve the productivity of businesses because business people could make spending and investment decisions without having to consider the tax consequences.

On the other hand, people who oppose the flat-rate tax argue that it would mainly help the wealthy by transferring more of the tax burden to middle- and lower-income people.


Questions

1.  What is the major source of federal government revenue?

2.  What are the advantages and disadvantages of a progressive income tax?

3.  Is the flat-rate tax a regressive tax? Explain.

4.  Refer to the Authors' Commentary on page 591 of your text. Do you think a value added tax is preferable to a flat-rate tax? Why or why not?

Test Your Business Vocabulary

1. M (p. 579)    7. J (p. 594)
2. N (p. 580)    8. K (p. 594)
3. B (p. 588)    9. G (p. 597)
4. C (p. 590)   10. L (p. 595)
5. I (p. 591)   11. E (p. 595)
6. D (p. 593)   12. H (p. 595)

Programmed Review
(refer to the indicated pages
in the text)

1.
   A. (p. 574)
   B. (p. 576)
2.
   A. (p. 574)
   B. (p. 574)
3.
   A. (p. 578)
   B. (p. 578)
   C. (p. 578)
4.
   A. (p. 579)
   B. (p. 580)
5.
   A. (p. 588)
   B. (p. 588)
6.
   A. (p. 583)
   B. (p. 581)

7.
   A. (p. 590)
   B. (p. 591)
8.
   A. (pp. 594-595)
   B. (p. 594)
9.
   A. (p. 595)
   B. (p. 595)
10.
   A. (p. 595)
   B. (p. 595)
11.
   A. (p. 597)
   B. (p. 597)
   C. (p. 597)

Test Yourself (Multiple Choice)

 1. A (p. 588)
 2. C (p. 591)
 3. B (p. 587)
 4. D (p. 594)
 5. C (p. 595)
 6. A (p. 593)
 7. D (p. 579)
 8. B (p. 593)
 9. A (p. 597)
10. D (p. 595)

Exercise 19-3

1. (pp. 593-594)
2. (pp. 594-595)
3. (P. 595)
4. (p. 595)
5. (p. 595)
6. (p. 596)
7. (p. 597)

Exercise 19-4

A-5  bailment (p. 595)
B-1  antitrust (p. 588)
C-4  voluntary (p. 579)
D-6  consideration (p. 594)
E-10 consent (p. 580)
F-9  UCC (p. 597)
G-7  real property (p. 595)
H-2  progressive (p. 590)
I-8  express warranty (p. 596)
J-3  administrative (p. 579)

Test Yourself (True-False)

 1. True (p. 597)
 2. True (p. 594)
 3. False (p. 579)
 4. False (p. 590)
 5. False (p. 588)
 6. True (p. 577)
 7. True (p. 579)
 8. True (p. 573)
 9. False (pp. 581-584)
10. True (p. 585)

# CHAPTER 20

# Society, Technology,
# and Business

In order for business firms to be successful in the long run, they must adapt to the various changes in society and technology. Decision makers must adapt to changes in values and lifestyles. Specific changes in education, income, age, and family structure will dictate future courses of action for business firms. Changes in these basic areas will directly impact on the goods and services offered for sale and the strategies, policies, and procedures developed by business firms.

Another key section in this chapter covers the social responsibility of business. Social responsibility recognizes that managers represent the interests of stockholders, customers, employees, and the general public. The increasing interest in a public-private partnership in developing solutions to social problems is an indication of acceptance of the social responsibility concept.

The final section focuses on the impact of changing technology. The high standard of living that we enjoy depends on our desire and ability to pursue the benefits of changing technology. Business decisions are also influenced by technological advancements. The rapidity of these advancements requires that firms keep abreast of new ideas and inventions.

TEST YOUR BUSINESS VOCABULARY

Test your business vocabulary by matching each key concept with the appropriate phrase. Check your answers with those at the end of this chapter.

Key Concepts

____ 1. technology
____ 2. military-industrial complex
____ 3. "blue skies" unit
____ 4. zero population growth

____ 5. public-private partnership
____ 6. professional-managerial ethic
____ 7. traditional business ethic
____ 8. technology forecasting

Phrases

A. business owes it to society only to seek profit
B. the application of science so that people can do entirely new things or do old things in a better way
C. drawing on the special experience of private businesses, unions, and community organizations to join with government in solving social problems
D. decisions are weighed in terms of longer-range company welfare, not immediate profit
E. powerful network of military planners and industrial firms that influences the use of our country's resources
F. the birthrate that stabilizes the population level
G. a group responsible for bringing new ideas about the operations of a firm to its management
H. it involves gathering and interpreting all evidence of scientific advances


PROGRAMMED REVIEW

(To help you in understanding the chapter material and to see if you have mastered the objectives stated at the beginning of the chapter)

1. *Show how businesses can deal with change.*

   A. A _____ _____ unit is a special unit or committee responsible for bringing new ideas about the operations of a firm to its management.

   B. _____ _____ is a special technique used to deal with the fast rate of technological change.

2. *Describe population growth and regional shifts from 1970 to 1980.*

   A. _____ _____ _____ formation is the number of new households formed less the number dissolved in a year.

273

B. The _____ has grown consistently and rapidly, in contrast to the Northeast and the North Central regions.

3. *Describe the major projected changes in the United States' birthrate, income distribution, educational attainment, and sex composition of the workforce.*

   A. The U.S. is very close to realizing _____ _____

   _____, which is the birthrate that stabilizes the population level.

   B. The age distribution of the population can be explained in part by the increased _____ of our citizens.

4. *Give examples of the impact of the changing population on business planning.*

   A. The rising education level is important for business both in terms of the _____ force that will be available and in terms of the tastes of future customers.

   B. Managers need to know the _____ and the distribution of income in their market areas.

5. *Discuss changes which have occurred in American values since 1900.*

   A. Debt, leisure, and self-_____ are no longer considered sinful, but are now a major part of our national character.

   B. More women are working, and a greater percentage of them are working in _____ and _____ jobs.

6. *Distinguish between the traditional business ethic and the professional-managerial ethic.*

   A. The traditional business ethic says that business owes it to society only to seek _____.

   B. According to the professional-managerial ethic, managers represent the interests of stockholders, _____, employees, and the _____ _____.

7. *Evaluate the potential for public-private partnerships in solving social ills.*

   A. The Committee for Economic Development has made a good case for a public-private partnership to attack the problem of finding jobs for the _____-to-_____.

B.  The public-private partnership involves a joint effort between businesses, unions, community groups, and the _____.

8.  *Show how our nation has adjusted to the energy shortage.*

    A.  Data on energy usage shows that rising prices of crude oil resulted in great _____ in use of energy and in an increase in production of energy from other than imported fuel.

    B.  Business decision _____ has been greatly influenced by changes in the energy picture.

9.  *Show how changing technology affects the need for businesses to plan.*

    A.  Because of the rapid change in technology, it is important to the long-term success of the firm that the organization not define its objectives too _____.

    B.  Technological obsolescence encourages firms to reduce the _____ of obsolescence by introducing their own new products.

10. *Define the military-industrial complex and show how it relates to research and development in the United States.*

    A.  The military-industrial complex is a network of military _____ and industrial firms that influences the use of resources and guides research and development.

    B.  Our recent history of _____ and _____ wars has led to the birth and growth of the military-industrial complex.

TEST YOURSELF (Multiple Choice)

Test yourself by selecting the best answer.  Check your answers with those at the end of this chapter.

1.  A special technique used to deal with the rate of technological change is called:

    A.  "blue sky" forecasting
    B.  technology forecasting
    C.  economic forecasting
    D.  financial forecasting

2.  Which of the following is an accurate statement about population growth in the United States?

A. The population grew from 152 million in 1950 to 227 million by 1980.
B. The population grew from 100 million in 1950 to 326.5 million in 1980.
C. The rate of growth since 1970 was 29 percent per year.
D. The rate of growth since 1975 was 49 percent per year.

3. Zero population growth:

A. will never be reached in the U.S.
B. does not affect the demand for goods and services
C. is the birthrate that stabilizes the population level
D. was reached in 1981

4. The traditional business ethic says that firms owe it to society to seek:

A. satisfaction
B. utility
C. economies of scale
D. profit

5. Which one of the following phrases is inconsistent with the professional-managerial ethic?

A. protectionism
B. internationalism
C. government-business partnership
D. firms serve stockholders, customers, and citizens

6. The replacement of a technical product or product feature by a newer, better, or cheaper one is known as:

A. product obsolescence
B. engineering obsolescence
C. technological obsolescence
D. cybernetic obsolescence

7. Which of the following is not consistent with the Protestant ethic?

A. The Protestant ethic is a set of beliefs that dominated the lives of Americans from the time we became a nation until the present time.
B. It emphasizes a strong sense of duty and self-discipline.
C. It reinforces the profit motive.
D. It de-emphasizes hard work and thrift.

8. Which one of the following statements is false?

A. Our history of "cold" and "hot" wars has led to the growth of the military-industrial complex.

276

B. There is no relationship between the military-industrial complex and the nation's research and development efforts in terms of who conducts it and who pays for it.
C. A partnership of private industry and government is essential to provide for our nation's defense.
D. Research and development can lengthen a product life cycle.

9. Blue skies units:

   A. are responsible for bringing new ideas about the operations of a firm to its management
   B. concentrate on past activities
   C. normally do not report to the president
   D. are established outside of the organization

10. Which one of these statements is <u>not</u> true?

    A. The net annual household formation is the number of new households formed in a year less the number dissolved in that year.
    B. The net annual household formation rate is not a function of marriages and divorces.
    C. Married couples represented a sharply declining proportion of all households from 1960 to 1980.
    D. The net annual household formation rate is important to business planners.


TEST YOURSELF (True-False)

Test yourself by answering whether the following statements are true or false. Check your answers with those at the end of this chapter.

___ 1. The level of educational attainment has always been a major factor to consider in business planning.

___ 2. Many large firms use the services of "think tanks" for major future-oriented problem-solving.

___ 3. The key focus of the professional-managerial ethic is profit.

___ 4. Job-creation is an important by-product of the motive for profit which underlies the capitalist risk taking.

___ 5. Communication is the application of science so that people can do entirely new things or do old things in a better way.

___ 6. The public-private partnership is not an alternative in solving social problems.

___ 7. On a geographic regional basis, the population changes have been uneven in the United States in recent years.

___ 8. The U.S. has already realized zero population growth.

___ 9. The net annual household formation rate is important in business planning.

___ 10. The income distribution is essential information for firms selling consumer goods.

EXERCISE 20-1

(To improve your understanding of how technology affects business decisions)

1. Define the following concepts.

    a. technology

    b. technological obsolescence

    c. think tanks

2. What is the relationship between technology and the need to plan?

3. What is the relationship between technology and social problems?

EXERCISE 20-2

(To help you understand the social responsibility of business)

Indicate with an X whether the characteristics listed on the left are more closely associated with the traditional business ethic or with the professional-managerial ethic.

|  | Traditional business ethic | Professional- managerial ethic |
|---|---|---|
| 1. Internationalism | | |
| 2. Stockholder-oriented | | |
| 3. Protectionism | | |
| 4. Satisfactory long-term profits | | |
| 5. Maximum profits | | |
| 6. Government-business partnership | | |
| 7. Serves stockholders, customers, citizens, and employees | | |
| 8. Minimum government control | | |

EXERCISE 20-3

(To improve your understanding of various concepts related to society, technology, and business)

1. Discuss the importance of research and development in business planning.

2. What is the public-private partnership?

3. Why is the net annual household formation rate important to some firms?

4. What is zero population growth?

5. Why did the military-industrial complex evolve?

EXERCISE 20-4

(Scrambled Word Puzzle)

The letters for some of the key concepts from this chapter are scrambled on the left. Unscramble them and match each key concept with its definition somewhere in the right column.

1. HCETLONYOG

2. SIEKSNIUTEBUL

3. HTWORGZPROEPONOITAUL

4. IONLAITDRATSUBNISSEECIHT

5. TENNNAALUESUOHHOLDOORMAFNIT

6. LAISTRUDNIYRALITIMXLEPCOM

A. The birthrate that stabilizes the population level

B. The number of new households formed in a year less the number dissolved in that year

C. Business owes it to society only to seek profit

D. The application of science so that people can do entirely new things or do old things in a better way

E. A powerful network of military planners and industrial firms that influences the use of a large part of our nation's resources

F. A group responsible for bringing new ideas about the operations of a firm to its management

EXERCISE 20-5

(Incident:  Patents on Government-sponsored Research)


        The federal government is a major source of funding for research
and development.  It owns thousands of patents.  Prior to 1980, any
inventions that resulted from government-sponsored research were not
patentable by either universities or businesses.  This tended to discourage the commercial development of new products because the inventors
could not have exclusive rights to market them.
        In 1980, however, Congress passed a law that allows universities
and small businesses to keep patent rights to inventions they had
developed with federal research money.  More recently, the Senate
Commerce Committee and the House Science Committee approved bills that
would allow big businesses to do the same.

Questions


1.  Should the federal government support research and development?
    Why or why not?

2.  Do you think that big businesses should be treated the same as
    small businesses and universities with respect to patents that
    evolve out of government-sponsored research projects?  Why or why
    not?

# CHAPTER 20 ANSWERS

## Test Your Business Vocabulary

| | |
|---|---|
| 1. B (p. 617) | 5. C (p. 617) |
| 2. E (p. 622) | 6. D (p. 616) |
| 3. G (p. 602) | 7. A (p. 615) |
| 4. F (p. 607) | 8. H (p. 602) |

## Programmed Review
(refer to the indicated pages in the text)

| | |
|---|---|
| 1. | 6. |
| A. (p. 602) | A. (p. 615) |
| B. (p. 605) | B. (p. 616) |
| 2. | 7. |
| A. (p. 606) | A. (p. 617) |
| B. (p. 605) | B. (p. 617) |
| 3. | 8. |
| A. (p. 607) | A. (p. 619) |
| B. (p. 608) | B. (p. 620) |
| 4. | 9. |
| A. (p. 609) | A. (p. 620) |
| B. (p. 609) | B. (p. 621) |
| 5. | 10. |
| A. (p. 612) | A. (p. 622) |
| B. (p. 612) | B. (p. 622) |

## Test Yourself (Multiple Choice)

| | |
|---|---|
| 1. B (p. 602) | 6. C (p. 620) |
| 2. A (pp. 603-605) | 7. D (p. 615) |
| 3. C (p. 607) | 8. B (p. 622) |
| 4. D (p. 615) | 9. A (p. 602) |
| 5. A (p. 615) | 10. B (p. 606) |

## Test Yourself (True-False)

1. True (p. 609)
2. True (p. 602)
3. False (p. 615)
4. True (p. 615)
5. False (p. 617)
6. False (p. 617)
7. True (p. 605)
8. False (p. 607)
9. True (p. 606)
10. True (p. 610)

## Exercise 20-2

Traditional business ethic - 2,3,5,8 (p. 615)
Professional-managerial ethic - 1,4,6,7, (p. 615)

## Exercise 20-4

1-D technology (p. 617)
2-F blue skies unit (p. 602)
3-A zero population growth (p. 607)
4-C traditional business ethic (p. 615)
5-B net annual household formation (p. 606)
6-E military industrial complex (p. 622)

# CHAPTER 21

# Your Career
# in Business

Chapter 21 is designed to acquaint you with the fundamentals of assessing your own career goals and developing methods that allow you to realize these goals. Many of your questions about acquiring the right job for you are answered in this chapter.

The starting point for job seekers is the assessment of career values. Different people have different values and orientations, which in turn influence how they evaluate alternative career opportunities. After determining values, individuals must seek sources of career information. This information will help you in selecting specific jobs, industries and geographical areas.

In conducting the actual job search one must prepare data sheets, résumés, letters of inquiry, and actually participate in job interviews. Individuals must take care and time in preparing these written documents because they communicate something about the person.

The final sections of the chapter discuss the mechanics of the interviewing process, and making the final choice of a job. The interview is an exercise in face-to-face communication. The job-seeker should plan and prepare for the interview by reading the appropriate information. When making the final choice, the job-selection formula provides a methodical process by which a decision can be made.

TEST YOUR BUSINESS VOCABULARY

Test your business vocabulary by matching each key concept with the appropriate phrase.  Check you answers with those at the end of this chapter.

Key Concepts

_____  1. career values
_____  2. student data sheet
_____  3. résumé
_____  4. letter of inquiry

Phrases

A.  those things you feel are important in selecting a job
B.  physical characteristics, such as strength and appearance
C.  sent to a firm asking about the possibility of securing a job
D.  a biographical summary of your education, experience, activities, interests, career goals, and so on
E.  published by the Department of Labor
F.  the same as a college interview form


PROGRAMMED REVIEW

(To help you in understanding the chapter material and to see if you have mastered the objectives stated at the beginning of the chapter)

1.  *Assess career opportunities in terms of the job marketplace and career values.*

    A.  By career values, we mean those things that you feel are

        _____ in selecting a career.

    B.  Some people desire to work in a certain industry, but have not

        selected a specific _____.

2.  *Identify sources of career information and summarize the general employment outlook for major classes of jobs and industries.*

    A.  The Department of _____ is a good source of information about the job market.

    B.  A good source of information about expected earnings, working conditions, and advancement in specific career areas is the

        Labor Department publication, the _____ Outlook Handbook.

286

C. According to projected changes in employment through 1990, an increase of over _____ million jobs is expected.

3. *Analyze job growth by geographical area of the United States.*

   A. Geographically, the _____ and the _____ are expected to continue their boom in economic growth while the huge population centers of the Midwest and Northeast continue to lag.

   B. The estimated average annual rate of employment growth from 1979 to 1990 will be _____ percent.

4. *Analyze a methodical system for self-evaluation and understanding in preparation for securing a job.*

   A. In evaluating yourself and preparing for job hunting, the individual must assess his or her abilities and _____.

   B. A skill that is needed in most jobs, particularly as you move up in a company, is the human _____ skill.

5. *Discuss the preparation of student data sheets, résumés, letters of inquiry, and the mechanics of taking job interviews.*

   A. A student data sheet, which is also known as a _____ _____ _____, is prepared by the student placement office and filled out by students who sign up for campus interviews.

   B. A _____ is a biographical summary of your education, experience, activities, interests, career goals, and so on.

   C. One important guideline for preparing your résumé is to keep it _____ and _____.

   D. A _____ _____ _____ is the first written contact with a prospective employer.

   E. An interview is an exercise in _____-_____-_____ communication.

6. *Tell what is involved in the formula approach to job selection.*

   A. The formula approach to job selection should not be looked upon as either _____ or fool-proof.

   B. The job selection formula is a systematic way of helping you choose between or among job _____.

TEST YOURSELF (Multiple Choice)

Test yourself by selecting the best answer.  Check your answers with those at the end of this chapter.

1.  The projected change in employment from 1978-1990 shows the largest increase in which one of the following areas?

    A.  farm workers
    B.  service workers, except private household
    C.  operatives
    D.  nonfarm laborers

2.  Which area of government is likely to have the best information about various jobs?

    A.  Department of Labor
    B.  Department of Defense
    C.  Department of State
    D.  Department of Transportation

3.  When considering the projected average annual percentage growth in different geographical regions, the highest growth rate is seen in:

    A.  Northeastern states
    B.  New England states
    C.  Midwestern states
    D.  Sunbelt states

4.  A student data sheet is also known as:

    A.  a résumé
    B.  a college interview form
    C.  a placement office form
    D.  a letter of recommendation

5.  Which one of the following statements is most accurate?

    A.  Your skills and interests are usually very different.
    B.  The first step in seeking a job is to utilize the job-selection formula.
    C.  Your skills and interests are usually closely related.
    D.  The letter of inquiry is sent after the job has been accepted.

6.  All of the following are good hints for a successful interviewing experience, except:

    A.  don't be nervous
    B.  gather information on the prospective employer
    C.  be on time
    D.  have no anxiety at all

7. Which of the following is not a part of the "Career Value Check-list?"

   A. Do you like meeting people?
   B. How often do you change jobs?
   C. Do you want to be your own boss?
   D. Do you expect high starting pay?

8. Probably the most important skill that is needed in most jobs, particularly as you move up in the organization is:

   A. human relations skills
   B. typing skills
   C. skill in calculation
   D. skills relating to memory and precise observation

9. A good source of job information is the:

   A. <u>Social Security Handbook</u>
   B. <u>Military-Industrial Guide</u>
   C. <u>Occupational Outlook Handbook</u>
   D. <u>Statistical Abstract of the United States</u>

10. Which one of the following most accurately represents the sequential stages in a thorough job search?

    A. complete credential file, complete résumé, do job interviews, and research these employers
    B. develop list of potential employers, research employers, complete credential file, and complete résumé
    C. complete résumé, complete credential file, complete student data sheet, and do job interviews
    D. complete credential file, complete résumé, sharpen interview skills, and develop a list of potential employers


TEST YOURSELF (True-False)

Test yourself by answering whether the following statements are true or false. Check your answers with those at the end of this chapter.

____ 1. One of the questions on the Career Value Checklist is "Do you want public recognition?"

____ 2. There is one best style and format for a résumé.

____ 3. The letter of inquiry introduces the applicant and is usually sent with a résumé.

____ 4. An interview is an exercise in face-to-face communication.

_____ 5. The annual rate of employment growth is uniform in all geographical regions of the country.

_____ 6. Individuals should avoid creating a résumé that appears crowded.

_____ 7. Skills relating to memory and precise observation are considered the most useful at upper levels of the organization.

_____ 8. The formula approach to job selection should not be looked upon as either automatic or fool-proof.

_____ 9. According to the job search time-line, a thorough, well-planned job search and selection process may take eleven weeks or more to complete.

_____ 10. Most college students have very specific career goals and values.

EXERCISE 21-1

(To stimulate your career preparation)

1.  Describe briefly:

    a.  Occupational Outlook Handbook

    b.  Encyclopedia of Careers and Vocational Guidance:

2.  Give two examples of each of the following:

    a.  clerical occupations:

    b.  computer and related occupations:

    c.  banking occupations:

    d.  insurance occupations:

    e.  administrative and related occupations:

    f.  sales occupations:

EXERCISE 21-2

(To stimulate your thinking about how to choose a job)

Suppose that you have gotten to the point of actually choosing a job. Think carefully about your career values.

1. List those career values that are important to you; list as many as you like, but list at least five.

2. Rank the above career values from most important to least important.

3. Assuming you had four job offers, how could you use your career value rankings to choose from among the jobs?

EXERCISE 21-3

(To improve yourself in contemporary business)

Answer on plain pieces of paper.

1. Write a one page report on your ideas about the ideal career.

2. Write and evaluate your own personal résumé.

3. Write a letter of inquiry for a job.

4. Prepare your personal job evaluation formula.

5. Using the most recent edition of the <u>Occupational Outlook Handbook</u>, prepare a one page summary of the job of your choice. In this summary include the nature of the work, working conditions, job out-look, and earnings.

EXERCISE 21-4

(To acquaint you with various concepts related to your career in business)

1. Discuss the geographical differences in the average annual rate of employment growth from 1979 to 1990.

2. Discuss the steps in the methodical system for self-evaluation and understanding in preparation for job hunting.

3. A survey of marketing/sales managers indicated that maturity, personal selling/sales management skills, and appearance are the top three criteria in judging applicants for marketing jobs. Why do you think these factors weighed so heavily?

EXERCISE 21-5

(Incident: Another Perspective on Careers)

Answer the questions on a plain piece of paper.


Of the 680 million people in India, only 23 million hold paying jobs. Two-thirds of the population live on subsistence farms. Despite these statistics, very few college courses emphasize skills that could enhance their students' employment prospects. Instead, the vast majority of the courses offered are in the humanities.

There also is little link between industry and universities in India. The universities do not engage in practical research to help India's industries. Many Indians believe that there is no incentive to engage in research or to develop new products. The idea of career-oriented education is also generally rejected.


Questions

1. How do you think your career values would compare to those of a college student in India?

2. How do you think a college student in India would react to the discussion of the job selection formula in Chapter 21 of the text?

3. How do you think the belief that India's industries are so protected from competition that there is no incentive to engage in research or to develop new products affects career opportunities?

# CHAPTER 21 ANSWERS

Test Your Business Vocabulary

1. A (p. 628)
2. F (p. 640)
3. D (p. 640)
4. C (p. 643)

Programmed Review
(refer to the indicated pages
in the text)

1.
   A. (p. 628)
   B. (p. 628)
2.
   A. (p. 628)
   B. (p. 629)
   C. (p. 628)
3.
   A. (p. 635)
   B. (p. 631)
4.
   A. (p. 635)
   B. (p. 638)
5.
   A. (p. 640)
   B. (p. 640)
   C. (p. 640)
   D. (p. 643)
   E. (p. 646)

6.
   A. (p. 652)
   B. (pp. 652-653)

Exercise 21-1

1. (p. 631)
2. (pp. 628-629)

Exercise 21-4

1. (pp. 631-635)
2. (p. 635)
3. (p. 637)

Test Yourself (True-False)

1. True (p. 636)
2. False (p. 640)
3. True (p. 643)
4. True (p. 646)
5. False (p. 631)
6. True (p. 640)
7. False (p. 638)
8. True (p. 652)
9. True (p. 650)
10. False (p. 636)

Test Yourself (Multiple Choice)

1. B (pp. 628-629)
2. A (p. 629)
3. D (p. 635)
4. B (p. 640)
5. C (p. 637)
6. D (p. 647)
7. B (p. 636)
8. A (p. 638)
9. C (p. 629)
10. D (p. 650)